What people are saying about

The British State

An outstanding primer about one of the most urgent issues of
the day.
John Pilger

This gripping, fast-paced and provocative book is an alternative
history of Britain. It shows how the carefully nurtured image
of British fair play and liberalism has in fact concealed the
real drama: the raw manipulation of power by and for a small
number of people. British capitalism has historically actively
undermined and suppressed any real change to the balance of
power: this book warns that a future progressive government
will face the same intransigence.
Brian Eno

Fascinating and insightful. A timely and important book.
Francesca Martinez

A concise, salutary and very valuable history. The state as it
really is not how it would like to appear.
Mike Wayne

Home Truths deftly told.
Danny Dorling

T0163432

The British State
A Warning

The British State
A Warning

Chris Nineham

Winchester, UK
Washington, USA

JOHN HUNT PUBLISHING

First published by Zero Books, 2019
Zero Books is an imprint of John Hunt Publishing Ltd., No. 3 East St., Alresford,
Hampshire SO24 9EE, UK
office@jhpbooks.com
www.johnhuntpublishing.com
www.zero-books.net

For distributor details and how to order please visit the 'Ordering' section on our website.

ISBN: 978 1 78904 329 7
978 1 78904 330 3 (ebook)
Library of Congress Control Number: 2019945254

A CIP catalogue record for this book is available from the British Library.

Design: Stuart Davies

UK: Printed and bound by CPI Group (UK) Ltd, Croydon, CR0 4YY
US: Printed and bound by Thomson-Shore, 7300 West Joy Road, Dexter, MI 48130

We operate a distinctive and ethical publishing philosophy in
all areas of our business, from our global network of authors to
production and worldwide distribution.

Contents

Acknowledgements

While I take responsibility for all the opinions it contains, I am indebted to many people for making this short book possible. Lindsey German, John Rees, Dave Randall and Des Freedman very kindly discussed it with me from start to finish and have given me crucial ideas, criticism and corrections. Dragan Plavsic provided some vital insights, Vladimir Unkovski-Korica, Michael Rosen, Elaine Graham-Leigh, Sofie Mason and Feyzi Ismail read later versions and gave invaluable feedback. Doug Lain at Zero Books has been generous in support and encouragement. Feyzi Ismail and Elaine Graham-Leigh were excellent sub-editors. More generally I have learnt a huge amount on the subject from my involvement with a wide range of activists and campaigners at the Stop the War Coalition, in the People's Assembly, in Counterfire and from the Labour Left. I hope what follows is a useful contribution to what is a more and more urgent discussion.

In all cases it must be remembered that a political combination of the lower classes, as such and for their own objects, is an evil of the first magnitude.
Walter Bagehot, The English Constitution, 1872[1]

Q: *I don't think he's got much clout in Whitehall, has he?*
A: *None at all. He's just a minister.*
Yes, Prime Minister, 1986[2]

Chapter One

Introduction: The Myth of Gradualism

In actual history, it is a notorious fact that conquest, enslavement, robbery, murder, in short, force, play the greatest part.
Karl Marx[3]

It is regarded as bad manners to discuss the British state. The word 'state' describes all the official bodies that govern our society. The existence of governing institutions beyond parliament is recognised, of course. But seeing unelected institutions like the police, the courts, the army, the civil service, the royal family and so on all as part of a 'state' implies they make up a system of rule. It has an undemocratic ring to it.

Even taken separately, there is little discussion about most state institutions. Parliament is in full view as the partially democratic element of the state. The royal family is also publicly celebrated as the official face of the nation, although its considerable powers and influence on politics are mostly passed over in silence. The civil service, which employs nearly 400,000 people in actually managing society, including its finances, is rarely discussed. Civil servants' meetings with politicians are confidential. The wide network of unelected, unaccountable 'quangos' linking government and business is barely mentioned. Lobbyists and private sector advisors play a more and more central role in the creation of policy. The situation is getting worse. A recent sympathetic account of how British government works admits, 'there are now far more participants than there used to be in the on-going Whitehall conversation. Unfortunately, not much is publicly known about some of them or what they have to say.'[4]

Despite Britain's jury system, legal practice is obscured

in a process based on expert interpretation of precedent. The parts of the state concerned with force are even more opaque. Police guidelines, priorities and strategy are decided in secret, largely by the police themselves. What public discussion there is about the military is limited to debates about funding and hardware. How the armed forces are run, their game plans and their discussions with elected politicians are kept out of the public domain. Nowadays mini-wars are fought without public knowledge on the basis that disclosure would endanger national security. The security services are the most private of all. Britain spends more on them than any other Western country apart from the USA. Mainly because of them we are the most monitored population outside China. Well over three million of us have DNA samples stored on computers. MI5 holds secret files on 272,000 individuals, equivalent to one in 160 adults.[5] Despite the scale of all this activity, it was only admitted in 1984 that the security services existed at all. Even cabinet ministers are not allowed to know what they do. When he was a cabinet minister in the 1970s, Tony Benn was told it was not his business to know if his own phone was being bugged.[6]

The reluctance to discuss many of the key institutions that actually manage society has a long history. Soon after the word 'state' gained its modern meaning in the sixteenth century, it tended to be replaced in English political thought by other concepts like 'commonwealth', 'political society' or 'civil society'.[7] In the words of a contemporary historian, 'the idea of the centrality of governments, rather than the state, of Westminster rather than Whitehall' is one of 'the most powerful assumptions of our national history'.[8]

Aside from the need to keep secrets from our enemies, the main justification for the low visibility of the unelected state is that it doesn't really matter. The argument runs that the history of Britain has been one of the gradual, organic expansion of liberty through compromise, with parliament as the emerging

2

democratic forum. Unlike in many other countries, so the story goes, the state has played no more than an enabling role in the evolution of our freedoms. The outcome is a parliamentary democracy with sensible checks and balances. The retro gothic architecture of the 'Palace of Westminster' is there to tell us that a democratic spirit has been with us since the middle ages. As a result, beyond the pomp of parliament and the harmless but comforting oversight of the monarchy, we have a small state made up of a set of neutral institutions whose role is simply to implement and guide the democratic decisions of our representatives. As one recent study puts it, our civil servants are 'impartial', 'uncorrupt and incorruptible' and the service as a whole is 'manifestly superior' to others.[9]

This short book will argue that this is history as myth. It sets out to challenge every element of it. It will argue that far from being neutral, the modern British state has consistently and often ruthlessly operated in the interests of the capitalist class. It will show that the state has developed not by gradual evolution, but through a series of struggles which have shaped it and the kind of society we live in. It will argue that portraying the development of British politics as organic or spontaneous obscures the fact that state institutions have been deliberately organised to maintain the status quo. But the book keeps coming back to a central paradox. Despite the partisan and oppressive history of British state rule, the idea of a neutral state and the gradual evolution of British freedoms has been influential, even on the Left. This confidence in our institutions has been one of the factors that has contributed to the state's survival.

Reluctant democrats

The myth of gradualism turns the history of the British state on its head. Far from being an organising principle of British development, democracy was a relative latecomer. The key institutions of the state, including parliament, emerged well before there was anything approaching a popular vote. The majority of the population got the vote in 1918 and it wasn't until 1928 that we had universal suffrage. So the 'mother of parliaments' only became fully democratic after the parliaments of 28 other countries. By this time, parliament in various elite incarnations had been in session for centuries. When the London police force was set up in 1829, only around 400,000 people had a vote in the whole country. When a recognisably modern civil service emerged in the second half of the nineteenth century, that number had risen, but only to 1.43 million out of a population of 30 million.

But it isn't just that the institutions of the modern state predate democracy. Despite British capitalism's origins in a revolution with strong democratic aspirations, the state that emerged in the second half of the seventeenth century actively obstructed further democratic change. When struggles for the popular vote re-emerged in the late eighteenth century, special constables, troops, and later police regularly attacked democracy campaigners. The courts followed through by imprisoning and deporting them in their thousands. Throughout the nineteenth century, almost all politicians in both houses of parliament were deeply committed to limiting the franchise to people of property and denying working people the vote. Democracy was the hard-won victory of mass campaigning. It is one of the ironies of British history that confrontational and sometimes revolutionary struggle has done a great deal to shape the very institutions that are supposed to embody British gradualness.

Democracy then was a late and bitterly opposed development in the history of the British state. But the idea of a limited, neutral state facilitating gradual change flies in the face of many other aspects of the historical record. It ignores the fact that the origins of the modern state lie in the seventeenth century revolution in which a monarch was tried for political crimes by his former subjects and executed. It erases the violent subjugation of

Ireland that followed, and the forced incorporation of Scotland and previous conquest of Wales, without which Britain could not exist. Its origin in conquest means that the British state is inherently coercive. The re-conquest of Ireland was not just brutal in itself, the subsequent occupation's basis in barbarity, but discrimination and chronic underdevelopment has ensured a legacy of struggle and sectarianism ever since, and kept violence at the heart of British state rule. The revolution of the 1640s and the Glorious Revolution that followed led to a massive increase in military mobilisation for foreign wars way beyond these islands. The need to increase military reach was in fact one of the factors that drove the revolution.[10] The British state since then has a historically unsurpassed record of war, pillage and occupation. Britain pioneered the slave trade, led the brutal colonisation of vast swathes of the globe and has fought energetically in wars against independence movements, uncooperative regimes and imperial competitors ever since.

No democracy could escape being compromised by such a record of war and oppression. It is only recently and as a result of popular pressure that parliament has adopted the habit of voting on questions of war. Collaborating with Foreign Secretary Ernest Bevin, the post-war Labour Prime Minister Clement Attlee committed Britain to a nuclear arms programme without consulting the cabinet, let alone parliament. The state more generally is structured on military and imperial assumptions. The Foreign Office and the Ministry of Defence cling on to neo-colonial fantasies, the monarchy embodies imperial tradition and the military and the security services play a central role in the British polity. In the words of John Le Carre, 'our security services are still, for better or worse, the spiritual home of our political, social and industrial elite'.[11]

The democracy that finally emerged in the twentieth century was limited in a variety of other ways. Parliament embodies a sharp division in society between politics and economics and we shall see that this is a division that is carefully policed by the elites. Economic issues, including how much people earn, property rights and levels of inequality are mostly outside parliamentary jurisdiction. For a few decades after World War Two, some socially-based intervention in the economy was grudgingly accepted. But the last 4 decades has been the history of elite pushback against this mid-century crossing of red lines. Nowadays the state's economic role is tightly focussed on the maximisation of profits. Parliament is surrounded by undemocratic institutions with more decision-making power than is normally admitted. Far from being neutral, the Whitehall ministries are controlled and staffed by people with clear ideas of how society should be run. The fear and contempt for democracy on display in nineteenth-century state institutions lives on in the threats and warnings from business organisations, the media, civil servants and the military about the dangers of a left-wing government today.

The nature and behaviour of the British state is now a question of immediate concern. For the first time in decades there is a chance that a party with a radical social democratic and anti-war leader could soon be heading up the government of a country whose elites are mostly confirmed neoliberals and foreign policy hawks. Getting Jeremy Corbyn's government elected in these circumstances is in itself a major challenge. But as Ralph Miliband wrote about a similar situation elsewhere, 'the really important question is what happens then'.[12]

Another reason to open up discussion on the record of the British state is that it is suffering a growing crisis of legitimacy. Politicians in Britain are now famously trusted less than estate agents and confidence in key institutions of the state is in long-term decline.[13] A central explanation for this is that the political elite's embrace of neoliberalism has been accompanied by the stripping away of welfare, the state's growing integration with big business and the adoption of more authoritarian, punitive attitudes. These developments demand analysis not just for the difficulties they pose for any reform project but for the possibilities they raise for change.

Despite this, even on the Left, the record, nature and evolution of our state institutions remain largely undiscussed. A recent collection of alternative economic proposals edited by the shadow chancellor barely touches on the difficulties that state institutions would pose for their implementation.[14] On the rare occasions when such questions are discussed on the Left, attitudes are often surprisingly relaxed. Fears of financial sabotage, Whitehall obstruction or security service destabilisation tend to be discounted. In Paul Mason's words, 'the "very British coup" scenario is a non-starter'.[15] Most radical commentators are assuming that the institutions of the state will bend to the will of a radical government and that the dominant interests in society will be happy to do what they are told. This book is a warning against such complacency, and a call for preparations for a much rougher ride.

The vanishing state

Emphasis on gradual change and the tendency to downplay the role of the state are both features of most 'advanced' capitalist societies. Perhaps surprisingly at first sight, the best explanation for this comes from the intellectual tradition which insists the most on the state's partisan role. Karl Marx argued that the executive of the modern state is 'but a committee for managing the common affairs of the whole bourgeoisie'.[16] But Marx had a sophisticated view of the state. Historically, he argued, the state arose out of the need increasingly complex societies had to take care of tasks which could no longer be performed by the community at large. This included resolving internal conflicts, confronting outside enemies and producing and maintaining the means for survival and reproduction. But as the emergence of the state depended on society producing a surplus, it would

7

inevitably also be a vehicle for defending the interests of those who controlled it. So, under capitalism, Marx says, 'the bourgeois pay their state well and make their nation pay for it in order to be able without danger to pay poorly'.[17]

This dual function of the state and the fact that it partly plays a socially-useful role is one of the reasons why people can believe in its neutrality. But there are others. In previous societies, class rule was transparent. Under feudalism, for example, economics and political rule were fused. Feudal monarchs and lords, in return for some basic protections, physically commandeered a proportion of the produce from the peasants who owned the land in the areas they controlled. Capitalism works differently. Most people are dependent on going to work to 'make a living', and it is at work that a surplus is produced. The compulsion to work built into this economic arrangement and the fact that it is organised by private companies means that the state doesn't need to be involved in the day-to-day relations between capitalists and workers. As Marx noted, early supporters of capitalism were well aware of the advantages of this 'organic' form of exploitation. He quotes the English economist Joseph Townsend: 'Legal constraint to labour is attended with too much trouble, violence and noise, creates ill will etc., whereas hunger is not only a peaceable, silent, unremitted pressure, but as the most natural motive to industry and labour, it calls forth the most powerful exertions.'[18]

The state's apparent lack of involvement in the economy allows it to appear to stand above society. Politics becomes a separate sphere in which the state deals with the population as abstract individual citizens rather than as economic actors and members of classes. This illusory separation between politics and economics is one of the secrets to working people's lack of control over society.

The state and the Left

A model of gradual change has dominated the British Left since the end of the nineteenth century. Internationally, many socialist parties were founded on the basis of hostility to capitalism and its institutions. This attitude often evaporated on contact with the enemy, but it was at least a formal opposition to capitalism. The British Labour Party, on the other hand, came into being explicitly committed to working for piecemeal change within existing structures. Questions of power were deliberately downplayed. The views of one of the Party's early leaders, Phillip Snowden, were typical of Labour's mainstream:

> The Labour Party is not seeking any class triumph. Its object is not to make the manual labour class dominant... it is quite true that the Labour and Socialist Party makes its appeal to the wage earning classes. It does so because there are people who need to be aroused to a fuller sense of civic duty... as they are the vast majority of the electorate they must exercise their political influence.[19]

Even more radical Labour leaders sought change by consensus. Keir Hardie, who had founded the openly socialist Independent Labour Party in 1893, explained in 1904 that, 'I can imagine one reform after another being won until in the end socialism itself causes no more excitement than did the extinction of landlordism in Ireland a year ago.'[20] The Labour Party hasn't deviated from this basic strategy since. Because of this and because of its limited successes, it has played a very important role in sustaining faith in the neutrality of the British state and the plausibility of a strategy of gradual change.

This strategy has not gone unchallenged. It was threatened in the run up to the First World War by a wave of strikes, some of whose leaders believed that workers could break the structures of power through militant trade unionism. The formation of the

Communist Party in 1920 popularised more radical critiques. The ideas outlined in Lenin's great defence of Marx's attitude to the state, *State and Revolution*, was for some time influential amongst thousands of working-class activists. Drawing together for the first time Marx and Engels' scattered remarks on the state and state power, Lenin argued that the state's very existence was the product of the irreconcilability of classes. Even when it played a partly mediating role, this was to defend the status quo. 'According to Marx,' he wrote, 'the state is an organ of class rule, an organ for the oppression of one class by another; it is the creation of "order", which legalizes and perpetuates this oppression by moderating the conflict between classes.'[21]

In the 1930s, influenced by the Communist Party and by their own frustrating experience, leading Labour Party intellectuals Stafford Cripps and R.H. Tawney developed searing critiques of the way the state works, although they remained committed to trying to work within it. Pressure grew for Labour to adopt a programme for the radical overhaul of the economy in these years. But the reforming achievements of the Attlee government after the Second World War confirmed government intervention in a mixed economy as the dominant strategy for change. While a lot of work was put into economic modelling, there was little discussion about the means to actually implement Left policy. In the words of Harold Wilson when he was at the Board of Trade in 1950, 'the problem of the relationship between the Government and Private industry is almost a vacuum in Socialist thought'.[22]

While the British Communist Party itself officially abandoned revolution and adopted a left reform strategy in 1956, the radicalisation of the 1960s and 1970s led to the revival of revolutionary ideas and renewed discussion about the state in which Marxist ideas had a strong influence. It was the publication of Ralph Miliband's book *The State in Capitalist Society* in 1969 and the subsequent debate with Nicos Poulantzas that focussed minds on the question. Miliband made the case once again, extremely controversial in social science at the time, that the state actively promoted the interests of the capitalist class and that it had the power to impose ruling-class interests independently of parliament, 'The fact that the government does speak in the name of the state and is formally *invested* with state power,' he wrote, 'does not mean that it effectively *controls* that power.'[23] Nicos Poulantzas criticised what he saw as Miliband's 'instrumentalism' and argued that the state was shaped by the structure of a more disembodied capitalism. Its most important role was to overcome capitalism's contradictions as a 'regulating factor of its global equilibrium as a system'.[24] Amongst Poulantzas' conclusions was the idea that the state could be subverted from within.[25] Miliband and Poulantzas were the most widely read social scientists of the time, but as we shall see, despite the significant growth of the revolutionary Left, and an upsurge of working-class militancy in the 1970s, the strategy of supporting a Labour government working through the institutions remained dominant.

The rise of Thatcherism led to a new round of discussion. This was often informed by the English publication of the *Prison Notebooks* by Italian revolutionary Antonio Gramsci. Along with Lenin's *State and Revolution*, the *Notebooks* contain the most important analysis of state power from the great revolutionary period of the early twentieth century. Paradoxically, they have often been used to advocate various ways of working within the system. In the *Notebooks*, Gramsci is preoccupied with the question of how socialists can build influence and power in Western capitalist countries in which the state had deepened its roots. His ideas were taken up in the 1980s, in a period of working-class defeat, to argue that the complexity and dominance of the modern state made ideas of insurgent change from below obsolete. The argument went that the working class was so decisively incorporated into the political process and market relations that the Left had to adapt by finding new allies and new ways of working within the institutions.[26]

Since that time Thatcher and her neoliberal successors have scored a remarkable success in convincing the mainstream that state intervention in the economy is ineffective and that the state is no longer a major player. As historian John Brewer argues, there was a concerted effort in the Thatcher years to prove that the state intervention of the period between 1945 and 1979 was 'a temporary diversion from the mainstream of the British political tradition'.[27] Globalisation reinforced this view. As a new study of the literature argues, some on the Left fell in with an emerging consensus, accepting the idea that:

> economic and financial internationalisation – what today we call 'globalisation' – had rendered the state increasingly powerless vis-a-vis the 'forces of the market' and that therefore countries had little choice but to abandon national economic strategies and all the instruments of intervention in the economy... and hope, at best, for transnational or supranational forms of economic governance.[28]

There are other ways in which neoliberalism's apparent hostility to the state has been internalised on parts of the Left. There is a habit, for example, of delinking power from class interest and seeing power as something that permeates the whole of lived experience. There is the tendency to retreat into a politics based on identity rather than on any strategy of actually trying to change society.[29] Various recent discussions of social change barely register the existence of state institutions let alone consider their conservative social role.

This book will show that the actual historical record reveals state institutions playing an active and vital part in the consolidation and defence of capitalism. As concessions to democratic and social movements became necessary in the second half of the nineteenth century, the more far-sighted representatives of the ruling class grasped that the appearance that core state institutions were neutral and 'above politics' was an advantage that could be exploited to defend the essentials of the status quo: the 'principle of property' in the words of Lord Balfour. But it didn't stop them or their successors from using force and fraud on a regular basis. These are not just matters of historical or academic interest. They are questions of immediate importance, because time after time the illusion of state neutrality has disarmed activists and allowed the relatively harmless incorporation of aspirations for change. We must not let this happen again.

The book is organised chronologically. The chapter which follows explores the state's role in the consolidation of capitalist rule achieved in the first half of the nineteenth century. It shows how free-market ideology was combined with ruthless state intervention to establish optimum conditions for capital accumulation. It also briefly describes the impressive and occasionally revolutionary resistance this process unleashed. Chapter Three discusses the ruling-class state makeover triggered by this turmoil. Fearful of losing control altogether, in the second half of the nineteenth century more clear-sighted members of the elite initiated a multi-level reform process designed to limit militancy and generate workable levels of consent. For all its strengths, this was a process that depended on the massive mobilisation of imperial violence abroad, but also on subjective weaknesses in the domestic Left. Chapter Four explores three moments of crisis in twentieth-century British capitalism. It shows that even in a period regarded as the golden age of gradual, consensual change, the full spectrum of state institutions were deployed to repress, criminalise and sabotage opposition movements inside and outside parliament. It discusses the state's flexibility in the face of aspirations for change, but also the extent to which the Labour Party's commitment to gradualism at all costs has helped to contain radical impulses. Chapter Five considers the reshaping of the state since Thatcher came to office. A refreshed free-market fanaticism was once more used to justify repressive state measures, involving open attacks on the right to protest and punitive social policies. The state was reorganised to strip away as much welfare infrastructure as possible and purge any sense of social responsibility that had developed. Market mechanisms and direct corporate control were the order of the day. The resulting state bristles with hostility at any suggestion of radical change. But the neoliberals are showing signs of fatal overreach. Many of the skills of what Chomsky has called manufacturing consent have been lost, and the British state is suffering from an unprecedented crisis of popular legitimacy. The concluding chapter looks at the implications of this record for radical politics today and tomorrow. It argues that the Left simply cannot afford to indulge the myth of gradualism any longer; that it is time to confront the difficult issues posed by the power of the state both in theory and in practice.

Chapter Two

Freeing the Market

Liberalism... is an act of will conscious of its own ends and not the spontaneous, automatic expression of an economic fact.[30]
Antonio Gramsci

A modern industrial capitalist state was consolidated in Britain during the first half of the nineteenth century. The regime it presided over was justified with a mix of traditionalism and free-market ideas but it was partly imposed with brutal force. Gradualism became ruling-class doctrine in response to the French Revolution of 1789. The revolution had re-energised the radical movements in Britain and panicked the British establishment. In response, governments brought in laws against 'seditious' meetings and writings and imprisoned radical printers and activists. But the British way had to be distinguished from the dangerous radicalism of the French. The Whig MP and writer Edmund Burke provided the key text. His hit pamphlet *Reflections on the Revolution in France* has provided many of the basic concepts for British conservatism ever since. Evoking natural processes, it pulled off the remarkable trick of linking liberty with property and prosperity with tradition. For Burke, British government:

> follows the pattern of nature, we receive, hold, and transmit our government and our privileges in the same way as we enjoy and transmit our property and our lives. The institutions of policy, the goods of fortune, and the gifts of providence are handed down to us, and from us, in the same course and order.[31]

Aspects of the way in which the British state had developed helped make this trick possible. The idea of gradual development was plausible partly because of the very earliness of the English Revolution of the 1640s and the lateness of the emergence of a democratic, bourgeois regime. The mid-seventeenth century revolution was a victory for merchants and a new class of commercial producers, some of them industrial, most of them still agricultural. Its democratic gains were rolled back later in the century and the full industrial capitalist take-off didn't happen until the 1830s. This time lag allowed the delinking of the emergence of industrial capitalism with the revolution. At the same time, the post-revolutionary ruling bloc of landowners, merchants and manufacturers suggested continuity. The landed aristocracy continued to play a leading role in political and public life right up until the end of the nineteenth century and universal suffrage wasn't achieved until well into the twentieth century. In the words of one historian this 'imparted to the British state its peculiar "feudal" colouration'.[32] But none of this should obscure the fact that Britain had become the global powerhouse of capitalist manufacturing by 1850.

There were differences between the manufacturing interests, bankers and landowners. Politically, these differences were roughly institutionalised by the Whig and Tory parties. Manufacturers and bankers tended to support the Whigs, the great landowners the Tories. During the nineteenth century the different factions of the ruling class had sharp disputes over a series of issues from trade tariffs to electoral reform. These disputes sometimes destabilised the state and opened up space for struggles from below, but they never led to irreconcilable conflict. Partly this was because the frightening radicalism of working people in Britain pushed the growing middle class into political agreement with the Tory aristocracy on questions of law and order. More fundamentally, it was because the aristocracy became more and more integrated into the capitalist economy.

As capitalism developed, earnings from landowning shot up. Landowners in the growing urban areas, or with holdings in coal-producing districts, found their incomes rose dramatically. Railway-building over aristocratic land was another major source of profit. The aristocracy soon started reinvesting the profits made from agriculture and other sources into the burgeoning capitalist economy. Many capitalist manufacturers on the other hand bought into land and liked to surround themselves with aristocratic trappings.[33]

The result was a state with institutions largely controlled by the aristocracy until the reform act of 1832, and still dominated by aristocrats for many years after. Landowners dominated parliament until the end of the century, the diplomatic service remained the preserve of the aristocracy until well into the twentieth century, and leading positions in the civil service only began to be opened up to some non-aristocrats in the 1870s. But it was a state run in general in the interests of capitalist accumulation. This is underlined by the fact that influential ruling-class figures recognised that the apparent dominance of the aristocracy could be useful in maintaining the rule of capital. Constitutional expert Walter Bagehot, for example, argued that the veneer of aristocratic rule suggested continuity, created a sense of awe in the population, and distracted attention from the nature of the real, 'efficient' political work going on.[34]

The other main element of early capitalist propaganda was the ideology of the free market. At the beginning of the nineteenth century, aristocratic British families began sending their sons for a season in Edinburgh instead of on the grand European tour. They sent them above all to be taught the ideas of Scottish economist and philosopher Adam Smith. Smith, who had died in 1790, was a complex writer but after his death his ideas were simplified.[35] In the stripped-down version, the 'rational' market choices of individuals led directly to a rational society. If state involvement in government was kept to an absolute minimum the free market would become a 'hidden hand' guiding the whole of society. Man, Smith had argued, 'by pursuing his own interests… frequently pursues the interests of society more effectually than when he really intends to promote it'. Free-market ideas spread quickly in ruling circles. Agricultural interests fought a rear-guard action against the repeal of the most important trade tariff, the Corn Laws, in the 1840s. But their defeat and the repeal of the Corn Laws in 1846 was final confirmation that capitalist manufacturing interests were in control.

Force and freedom

From the ruling-classes' point of view, both Burke's conservatism and Smith's free-market theories had the advantage of writing human agency out of history and downplaying the role of the state. But a brief examination of the parliamentary record shows that in fact the British state played an active and often ruthless role in creating the conditions for the development of capitalism. From the eighteenth century onwards, parliament finished the job of enclosing land that had either been owned by smallholders or regarded as common. Between 1760 and 1870, about seven million acres, nearly one-sixth the area of England, was transferred from common land to enclosed land by some 4,000 acts of parliament.[36] This often brutal process of what E.P Thompson called 'class-based robbery' had the double effect of concentrating land in the hands of the big landowners and of forcing landless and small peasants out of the countryside and into the pool of 'free labour' in the cities.

The existing system of poor relief also had to be scrapped to create the conditions for capital accumulation. From the time of the Tudors, provisions had been made for local parishes to provide support for the destitute or low-paid. Now the ruling elites needed to dismantle this system to relieve tax payers of an 'unnecessary' burden and, more importantly, to remove an artificial floor for wage rates. A Royal Commission of 1834 argued that poor relief should only be given to people in workhouses and that rates should be set lower than the wages of the lowest paid in employment. Many of the Commission's proposals were enacted in the new Poor Law of 1834, including restricting state benefit payments to male wage-labourers. These measures were deeply unpopular and sparked widespread resistance.

The limited regulation of working life was also dismantled. Legislation affecting the number of hours worked and setting guidelines for wages was scrapped. Some new laws aimed at clearing away legal obstacles to exploitation, while others outlawed collective resistance. In the eighteenth century, people had begun to organise at work and take industrial action. But the Combination Acts of 1799 and 1800 made workplace organisation illegal.[37] These were followed by the Master and Servant Act of 1823, which brought together and updated in one piece of legislation many years of anti-labour laws. The aim was to strip away any lingering sense of mutual dependence between the classes and insist on the unchallenged control of the employer. The Act was explicitly biased in favour of the employers. An employer in breach of contract was only liable in a civil action, whereas an employee could be sentenced by a local magistrate to imprisonment or hard labour. The Master and Servant Act was used with great brutality for 50 years. There are no accurate statistics for the first half of the century, but we do know that between 1858 and 1875 there were on average around 10,000 prosecutions a year.[38]

The whole of the state was mobilised to impose this new order. A widely quoted judgment from 1823 shows that the legal profession understood perfectly the part it was expected to play to enable exploitation. An agricultural labourer on a yearly contract was dismissed because he had refused to work beyond his usual dinner break. The labourer lost his job and a year's pay. The judge's explanation speaks volumes:

If the plaintiff persists in refusing to obey his masters' orders I think he was warranted in turning him away... it may be hard upon the servant, but it would be extremely inconvenient if the servant was to set himself up to control his master in his domestic regulations such as the time of dinner... the question really comes to this, whether the master or the servant is to have supreme authority.[39]

The state also helped to accelerate the accumulation of capital in the hands of capitalist investors. New research has shown, for example, that a programme of payments to compensate slave owners for the loss of their 'property' after abolition in 1833 gave a massive impetus to commercial development. Twenty million pounds, a huge sum at the time, was paid out to 46,000 claimants who either owned slaves or benefited indirectly from their ownership. Most of this money ended up funding new industrial and commercial projects and the development of the City and regional financial centres. At least four million pounds of this went into the development of the railway system, so crucial to industrial capitalism's mid-century take-off.[40]

The new order faced challenges way beyond the workplace. The French Revolution's promotion of universal human rights, equality and political participation had generated new perspectives and new forms of organisation amongst working people. Jacobin clubs and 'corresponding societies' spread widely in artisan communities. The demand for universal suffrage was revived. Various forms of agitation and unrest followed, including cycles of mass meetings, demonstrations and food riots. From 1811, the Luddite movement spread through northern industrial districts leading to the smashing of machinery on a massive scale. An account from 1816 suggests an insurrectionary mood in the country:

In London and Westminster riots ensued, and were continued

for several days whilst the (Corn) Bill was discussed; at Bridgeport there were riots on account of the high price of bread; at Bideford, there were similar disturbances to prevent the exploitation of grain; at Bury, by the unemployed, to destroy machinery; at Ely, not suppressed without bloodshed; at Newcastle-on-Tyne, by colliers and others; at Glasgow, where blood was shed; at Preston by unemployed workers; at Nottingham by Luddites, who destroyed 30 frames; at Merthyr Tydfil on a reduction of wages; at Birmingham, by the unemployed; and at Dundee where, owing to the high price of meal, upwards of one hundred shops were plundered.[41]

The main ruling-class response was to strengthen repression. Up to this point, to control disorder they had relied on a combination of locally recruited irregular police and special constables, with army back-up when things got serious. The scale of the disturbances stretched this arrangement to breaking point. Local constables were often unable to maintain control. The army took a long time to deploy from their bases and billeting in local households ran the risk of alienating local populations or of fraternisation. The result was an ambitious barrack building programme. A total of 155 barracks were built in the most disaffected areas, including one for 138,000 soldiers in London's Regent's Park, another for 82,000 in Liverpool, and bases for 60,000 in Bristol and 20,000 in Brighton.[42]

The Peterloo Massacre of 1819 underlined the state's reliance on violence but also showed that this programme had failed to solve the problem of repression. In the first months of the year there was growing agitation for electoral reform, leading to enormous working-class political gatherings across the country. In August, 60,000 people gathered to protest in St Peter's Field in Manchester, a city with a population of 20,000 without a single MP. Local magistrates called on the part-time soldiers of the yeomanry to arrest the organisers. The inexperienced, amateur yeomanry charged and succeeded in arresting the main speaker, Henry Hunt. But they failed to clear the protestors, their lines broke up and they had problems extricating themselves. The military commander ordered the 15th Hussars to intervene and clear the crowd. The Hussars charged with sabres drawn, killed 18 people and wounded up to 700. Peterloo showed the British state relied on force as its number one control mechanism. There have been some attempts to blame the killing on mistakes made by a panicked magistracy. But correspondence between local law enforcers and the Home Secretary's office shows that 'shedding blood by the Law or the sword' to 'tranquilise' the country was official, national policy.[43] All the same, the massacre raised questions in ruling-class circles about whether a new force was needed that would be better suited than troops to dealing with riots and strikes. Reformers argued shooting people or slashing them to death was too crude a form of repression and should be used only as a last resort. A campaign was started for a new police force which would specialise in non-lethal force and arrest. Reformer and police champion Edwin Chadwick put the case for innovation in matter of fact terms:

> Of the military force, it may be observed that the private soldier has both his hands occupied with a musket with which his efficient action is by the infliction of death by firing or stabbing. The constable or policeman whose weapon is his truncheon or on desperate occasions a cutlass, has one hand at liberty to seize and hold his prisoner, whilst the other represses force by force.[44]

After a long opposition the Metropolitan Police Bill was voted through in 1829, setting up a police force in London. To get the Bill passed, Home Secretary Robert Peel had to agree that the Metropolitan Police would not be able to operate in the City of London, overcoming fears from bankers that their own behaviour might come under scrutiny.[45] The new police force had a number of social functions and adopted more. But it is important to remember that it was designed first and foremost to be used against protests, strikes and in case of social disorder. This explains why it was organised along military lines in divisions and companies. After new legislation, by the 1840s almost all large towns in Britain had police forces which, except at times of extreme disorder, were capable of dealing with local riots or disturbances.

Reform and revolution

By the 1830s, more enlightened members of the Whig elite had realised that state repression would have to be leavened with some democratic reform. But the history of franchise reform shows that it was only finally granted under extreme pressure and that the establishment's main concern was to make it as ineffective and limited as possible. The first Reform Act of 1832 began the process of transforming parliament from a corrupt forum for landed and commercial interests into something a little more representative. But the changes were pitiful. The electorate increased from 478,000 to 813,000, all men, out of a total population of around 14 million. The overwhelming majority were middle or upper-class, although for the first time some skilled workers got the vote. Even this marginal reform was won by mass agitation, which at times reached insurgent levels.

The movement was led initially by middle-class radicals like Henry Hunt and William Cobbett. Their case for reform was based on a mixture of self-interest and fear of more fundamental change. The agitation took place against the background of protests and riots in the country and discontent in Ireland which had been electrified by the French Revolution of 1830. Leading Whig Sir William Napier wrote to his wife in 1831 to say that 'in London men speak sedition openly in the clubs and secretly in the streets; every person is prepared or preparing for a great change'.[46] Radical MP Edward Davenport argued that the 'industrious classes' were suffering greatly and discontent had to be appeased 'before parliament loses the confidence of the people and before they take the means of reform into their own hands'.[47] Scottish Whig MP Francis Jeffrey summarised the strategy as being 'to detach the discontented and disenfranchised middle classes from the multitude'.[48] Despite these arguments, a Whig-sponsored reform bill was voted down by Tories in the Lords. This led to a new surge of protest throughout the country. Nottingham Castle was burnt to the ground. In Derby, angry crowds sacked the jail, released all the prisoners and roamed the streets for 4 days. For a week Bristol was in the hands of armed insurgents who besieged the assizes, burnt Queens Square, the Mansion House, the Custom House, the Bishop's Palace and all four prisons to the ground. Seventy people were killed before a military force from London pacified the city.[49]

The Whig government was split over how to deal with the Lords' intransigence and prevaricated for months. In the face of rejection from parliament and repression by the military, the middle-class radicals began to lose control of the movement. In London, members of the National Union of the Working Classes and Others started pressing for a month-long general strike to allow workers to take control of the government and all national resources.[50] They organised two massive demonstrations for manhood suffrage, the second of which numbered perhaps 100,000. In April the radical working-class paper the *Poor Man's Guardian* began publishing excerpts from a manual in street fighting.[51] In May, the Birmingham Political Union held a meeting of 200,000 people in support of reform, and there was talk of a massive march on London. A manufacturer had offered to supply the union with 10,000 muskets for a cheap price and there were signs that the police and the yeomanry could not be relied on to keep order.[52] The radical reformer

Francis Place later commented that 'we were within a moment of general rebellion', and that had the Bill not gone through there would have been barricades in the main cities and towns. If it had happened, such a rebellion 'would have been the act of the whole people to a greater extent than any which had ever before been accomplished'.[53]

It was this critical situation, this threat to the system of private property, that finally forced Lord Grey's Whig ministry to act. Grey insisted that electoral reform was necessary to head off disaster, but he had always been clear that the aim was not to start a gradual process of democratisation, but to kill off popular democratic aspirations once and for all. In November 1831 he told parliament: 'If any persons suppose that this Reform will lead to ulterior measures they are mistaken; for there is no one more decided against annual parliaments, universal suffrage and the ballot, than I am. My object is not to favour, but to put an end to such hopes and projects.'[54]

A few months later, Grey took the unprecedented measure of demanding the king allow him to appoint 60 new Lords to vote the Bill through. Even then the government conceded the minimum possible. It was clear what the liberal reformers wanted above all was the ability to trade freely without obstacles of birth, state interference or religious discrimination. Democracy for working people presented a positive threat to this project. The movement subsided for a period, but the outcome failed to satisfy most activists and was denounced by many working-class leaders and newspapers.

The Chartist challenge

In the years of disappointment that followed, radical ideas continued to circulate. A core of activists stayed together and formed the basis for a movement that openly equated the struggle for democracy with the need to transform society. In 1837 a meeting of more than 4,000 working people at the Crown and Anchor Pub on the Strand in London drew up a Charter for electoral reform. It demanded equal representation for all areas, universal male suffrage with no property qualifications, annual parliaments and vote by secret ballot to ensure an end to intimidation and the buying and selling of votes. The campaign of 'Chartism' that followed once again brought together radical liberals and more militant representatives of the working class. But the radicals tended to dominate. The 'physical force' wing believed that reform would have to be imposed on the government.

When parliament rejected the Charter in 1839, the rank and file took matters into their own hands. As the national Chartist convention met in Birmingham, there were clashes with the police across the country. The Home Office received reports of widespread arming and drilling. In November, a speaking tour of South Wales by the physical force orator Henry Vincent ended with his arrest and incarceration in Newport. The movement in Wales started preparing for an insurrection. A total of 20,000 people joined a march on Newport to release Vincent from jail, which aimed to spark similar uprisings around the country. Arrangements had been made to establish a British Republic in the wake of a wave of insurrections. In the end, only a minority of the marchers reached Newport and they were defeated after a gun battle with troops billeted at the Westgate Hotel. Even after this setback there was talk of a northern uprising.

Chartism re-emerged more militant than ever in the midst of a strike wave that shook Britain's manufacturing regions in 1842. The strike centred around the great mills of Lancashire but spread within a week to Glasgow, the Scottish coalfields and South Wales. Its delegate conference voted overwhelmingly to adopt the Charter. Threatened by a rapidly politicising strike movement, the state once again responded with co-ordinated violence. The national leaders were arrested at the conference, undermining the coherence of the strike wave, though militancy continued at a local level for weeks. Despite these setbacks, the movement had reached an impressive level of politics and radicalism. Its leaders were internationalists: the most prominent in London was a black man named William Cuffay, the son of a slave from St Kitts. The editor of the movement's main paper, the *Northern Star*, Feargus O'Connor, and Chartism's most important theorist, Bronterre O'Brien, were Irish. They enthusiastically supported national movements in Hungary, Poland and Canada and opposed slavery. Chartism revived again in 1848 in response to revolution in France. The February French uprising swept aside the monarchy of Louis-Phillipe in a day, instituted a democratic franchise and abolished slavery. It was met with rejoicing by republicans and revolutionaries everywhere, sparking a Europe-wide wave of uprisings. In England the revolutionary wave helped inspire a new round of protests coinciding with the third great Chartist petition.

In the run up to a national demonstration planned for 10 April 1848, there were real concerns in ruling circles about insurrection. On 8 April, Waterloo station was closed while hundreds of special constables helped evacuate Queen Victoria and the Royal Family to the Isle of Wight. The Chartists had planned a peaceful demonstration to Westminster, not a physical confrontation. The government, on the other hand, had laid careful plans for a show of strength. All public buildings were heavily guarded and all the bridges over the Thames were blocked. A total of 4,000 police, 150,000 special constables and 1,231 Enrolled Pensioners were joined by 7,122 troops, including cavalry.[55] Faced with this show of force, the Chartist leadership abandoned plans to march and the day was celebrated by the government as a victory over the movement.

Although unrest continued around the country for some months, this setback for the movement and growing panic amongst the middle classes about the possibility of revolution provided the elites with an opportunity for a decisive crackdown on the Chartist leadership. From June 1848, there was a co-ordinated wave of arrests of the key leaders of the movement. Hundreds were sentenced and deported. Combined with previous waves of arrests, imprisonments and deportations, this operation amounted to the effective crushing of the most advanced working-class movement anywhere on earth at the time.

This clampdown underlined the extent to which force was the central element of ruling-class control in the first half of the nineteenth century. As John Saville, one of the great socialist historians of the period, explained:

What has usually been missed in the analysis of historical change around the middle of the nineteenth century has been the physical destruction of the mass movement of working people by the now greatly enhanced efficiency of the coercive power of the British state. The mass imprisonment, transportation and successful confrontation of the mass demonstrations during the three main periods of the Chartist years contributed considerably to the disintegration of the national movement. Without that physical assault upon the militant sections of the Chartist leadership and so many of the second line activists, the aftermath in the 1850s might have been different.[56]

Far from emerging through compromise, the process of securing capitalist state power relied on coercive legislation backed up by the mobilisation of overwhelming force. In direct contradiction to the myth of the gradual emergence of democracy, the early political representatives of the capitalist class focussed their political energy on trying to block popular democratic aspirations for ever. Repeated rounds of physical repression were aimed above all at crushing movements of working people demanding the vote. The first Reform Act aimed to consolidate the ruling block by enfranchising its middle-class base as a bulwark against calls for universal suffrage.

The capitalists' success, however, was not inevitable. Marx and Engels were great champions of the Chartists, but they also pointed out the significance of some of the movement's weaknesses. They fully supported the democratic struggle, but they also warned of the risks involved in dealing with politics in isolation from social questions. In *The Conditions of the English Working Class*, Engels argued that it was a mistake for the Chartists to restrict their demands to the political. Doing so ignored the economic basis of ruling-class power and encouraged complacency about how ruthlessly the ruling class would defend its privileges. Engels also pointed forward to the fact that political liberty would not in itself transform social relations, 'The evil they suffered was social', he said, 'and social evils cannot be abolished as the monarchy or privileges are abolished.'[57] At times, the most radical Chartists understood that power would have to be seized and would never be granted. But despite various attempts, the movement ultimately failed to develop a strategy capable of rising to this task. In contrast, the ruling class had no qualms about the decisive use of force. The Chartists' hesitation in 1848 gave the regime the opening that it needed.

Chapter Three

Empire State

Reform that you may preserve.[58]
Thomas Macaulay

The Chartist movement never recovered from the anti-climax of 1848 and the repression that followed. But for all the establishment's success in crushing the democracy movement, there was a change of approach in ruling-class circles in the second half of the nineteenth century. The earlier cycles of mass popular resistance had convinced more far-sighted members of the elite that repression alone could not ensure capitalist stability. The elites were not suddenly converting to democracy or to opening up state institutions. Rather, they sensed the need to change the balance between force and consent so that in Gramsci's phrase, 'force will be made to appear to be based on the consent of the majority'.[59] These years in which the state began to take on something approaching its modern form were marked by a careful reform process, still accompanied by the systematic use of force but consciously designed to defuse opposition, incorporate some elements of the working-class movement and secure core state institutions against the dangers of democracy.

Up until the early 1840s, almost all measures relating to the workforce were repressive or penal. From mid-century, the state was partly re-orientated. There was a turn towards regulating exploitation, some social reform and strategies of co-option, accompanied by a strengthening of core state institutions. The reforms were consciously designed to limit the horizons of the working class. The journalist and constitutional expert Walter Bagehot expressed the new mindset of the establishment very clearly in the preface to his book on the British constitution. In a discussion of how to avoid the 'political combination' of the working classes he said of the rich:

> They must avoid not only every evil, but every appearance of evil; while they still have the power they must remove, not only every actual grievance, but, where it is possible, every seeming grievance too; they must willingly concede every claim they can safely concede, in order that they may not have to concede unwillingly some claim that would impair the safety of the country.[60]

He put the same point rather more directly in a later passage specifically referring to the House of Lords: 'They should give large donations out of income,' he said, 'and by so doing they keep, as they would keep, their capital intact.' Social reforms began falteringly in the 1840s. Between 1842 and 1850, parliament passed the Factory Act, the Coal Mines Act and the Ten Hour Act, all introducing minimal limits to exploitation. The Coal Mines Act, for example, banned boys under 10 years of age from working underground. This trend towards social reform accelerated after the Second Reform Act in 1867 significantly widened the franchise. One of the key steps was the development of a system of universal elementary education in the Education Act of 1870. This was partly motivated by the need for more skilled workers as manufacturing became increasingly complex and foreign competition intensified. Partly too as Britain had become the commercial and financial centre of the world and the hub of the world's greatest empire, it was necessary to train up more clerks and supervisory workers, and most of these had to be drawn from the working class. But the Act was also a response to the tendency of workers to educate themselves, which had reached disturbing levels during the high points of struggle in the previous decades when radical books and newspapers had been amongst the bestsellers.

The thinking behind these measures is well described in an 1856 pamphlet called *Employers and Employed*, a kind of handbook to mid-century liberalism. The book advocates 'nobler forms of authority' than 'sheer naked will', arguing that the most effective kinds of authority 'rest entirely on enlightened public opinion'. It moves easily from the realm of government to questions of 'factory rule', arguing that improving the lot of working people and treating them with respect actually strengthens class power:

> Precisely in proportion as working men and women shall stand erect before their employers, in the unassuming dignity of conscious intelligence and uprightness, so will the bearing of the latter become respectful, losing the tone and manner of command, yet consciously acquiring more and more of the reality of power.[61]

State-led reforms were supplemented and encouraged by a campaign of philanthropy. Urban industrialists and their supporters consciously sought to engage a section of the working class and promote the idea of self-improvement. One Halifax industrialist proudly told the Newcastle Commission on education in 1859 that he maintained and managed 'six day schools, five Sunday schools, two evening schools, and one working-men's college; also two public libraries, containing about 7,000 volumes, for the use of the working classes'.[62] These initiatives were designed to help incorporate and deradicalise at least more 'respectable' working people. A factory inspector's report from 1864 quotes a source from the Potteries as saying, 'I am proud... to say that Chartism is only known as a thing that was. Improved circumstances and better information have wiped out that stain from the character of the town forever.' The witness goes on to suggest that local reforms had had a profound ideological impact, noting that the people's 'tastes have been elevated, their ambitions excited, and a desire for progress has been turned into a proper channel. An onward march has been started in good earnest.'[63]

Efforts were made to integrate working people's representatives. Some employers began to recognise trade unions, particularly for skilled workers, and formal mechanisms for negotiation between management and unions began to emerge.[64] In 1850 the idea of a full-time union official was unknown; by 1891 there were 600.[65] This new trade union bureaucracy tended to have a restraining impact on the workforce. Meanwhile, the emergence of the Liberal Party under William Gladstone from an alliance of Whigs, Tory free traders and radical politicians helped to draw some working-class activists into the political process. One of the effects of what David Nicholls called 'the mystifying appearance of aristocratic hegemony' was that some workers could be won to identifying with a party focussing on moderate democratic and constitutional reform, even if it steered clear of working-class demands.[66] The first working-class MPs, Thomas Burt and Alexander MacDonald, both miners' officials, were elected as Liberals in 1874. By the 1870s even the trade union leaders who had sat with Marx on the General Council of the First International were concentrating their energies on the Liberal Party.[67]

As the century progressed, there was a change in the way leading liberal intellectuals discussed the state, a change accelerated by the extension of the franchise after 1867 and the return of militant class struggle in the 1880s. Driven by the need to provide a new social base for capitalist rule, the new ideology claimed a convergence of interest between the 'productive classes', meaning workers and capitalists. The state was no longer seen as merely intrusive but instead could help regulate the system so that everyone gained some benefit from economic growth. There was a recognition that enlightened self-interest didn't automatically create the best conditions for human development. In the words of one prominent liberal writer of the time, a society in which an honest and average worker cannot make ends meet 'is to that extent suffering from malorganisation'.[68]

Securing the state

These changes were accompanied by an overhaul and expansion of the civil service. Before the 1850s, the state was still being run by politicians' friends, careerists and various aristocratic misfits. Sir Edward Trevelyan and Sir Stafford Northcote produced a report in 1854 arguing for modernisation. They recommended recruitment examinations, a unified civil service, a sharp division between intellectual and 'mechanical' tasks, and an emphasis on the humanities rather than science in the selection of candidates for the top jobs. The report was not recommending meritocratic openness. It was taken for granted in the establishment that state administration was one area that should remain closed off to working people, however 'respectable'. Lord Trevelyan in particular was no democrat. He had trained in the brutal colonial administration in India and he was best known for denying food relief to starving victims of the Irish Potato Famine because 'the real evil with which we have to contend is not the physical evil of the Famine, but the moral evil of the selfish, perverse and turbulent character of the people'.[69]

Trevelyan and Northcote urged reform to protect the status quo. In the words of one historian of the period, their report was a response to 'the perceived need to put the running of the country in "safe hands" prior to the inevitable arrival of democracy'.[70] The report's authors understood that a professional, permanent civil service would be a powerful bulwark *against* democracy if it possessed, in their own words, 'sufficient independence, character, ability and experience to be able to advise, assist and to some extent influence those who are from time to time set over them'.

The aristocrats who dominated parliament rejected the reform proposals many times as a threat to their control of the ministries. It wasn't until 1870 that the report's full programme was implemented. The reforms led to the biggest ever peacetime expansion in the civil service, from 55,000 in 1873 to 280,000 by the First World War.[71] But while automatic aristocratic access to the civil service was ended, the reforms were carefully calibrated to institute a new form of elitism based on upbringing, values and educational background. The public schools and Oxford and Cambridge universities, both expanding in this period, provided in the words of one sociologist, 'a constant supply of new recruits who possessed the cultural attitudes and outlook appropriate for the continuation of the establishment and its "traditional social order".[72] One hundred years later, in 1970, nearly 70 per cent of top civil servants still had degrees from Oxford or Cambridge.[73]

Imperial boom

The economic context was crucial to the strategy of stabilisation. In his London Address to the International Workingmen's Association in 1863, Marx pointed out that the previous 20 years had seen a 300 per cent growth in British trade. This was the period in which Britain came to be called the workshop of the world. The working class as a whole had seen few of the benefits of this bonanza, in fact 'death by starvation rose almost to the rank of an institution during this intoxicating epoch of economical progress in the Metropolis of the British Empire'.[74] Life for workers remained miserable and, for the poorest, almost intolerable. But the sketchy economic records suggest that some workers saw improvements during the boom. On average, wages rose by a modest 33 per cent in real terms between 1850 and 1873. Skilled workers, including those in the cotton and building trade, and to a lesser extent engineers, shipbuilders and printers, benefited most.[75] Unskilled workers benefited much less from the boom, and there is no support in the statistics for the idea that any section of working-class people benefited spectacularly.[76] But the boom created a context in which some workers could win wage increases from their employers through sectional struggles.[77]

As Marx made clear, the boom wasn't just the result of free trade. It was made possible by the expansion and consolidation of Britain's colonial territories. In the century from 1815, around ten million square miles of territory and roughly 400 million people were added to the British Empire, often using extreme violence.[78] In 1858, the British government took over the East India Company and assumed direct control over India, establishing the British Raj. India became the empire's most valuable possession, 'the Jewel in the Crown'. Between 1875 and 1900 imperial expansion accelerated sharply as a result of the 'Scramble for Africa'.[79] The share of British exports going to empire markets surged throughout this period.[80] The link between empire and social control was explicit. As arch-imperialist Cecil Rhodes put it, 'If you want to avoid Civil war, you must become imperialists.' Russian revolutionary Leon Trotsky brilliantly expressed the conservative impact of these developments on British ruling-class thought and behaviour. Britain, he wrote:

was the pioneer of bourgeois civilization; she was not under the yoke of other nations, but on the contrary held them more and more under her yoke. She exploited the whole world. This softened the inner contradictions, accumulated conservatism, promoted an abundance and stability of fatty deposits in the form of a parasitic caste, in the form of a squirearchy, a monarchy, House of Lords, and the state church. Thanks to this exclusive historic privilege of development possessed by bourgeois England, conservatism combined with elasticity passed over from her institutions into her moral fibre.[81]

The return of the repressed

Colonialism provided the context for an increasingly racist version of English nationalism, which helped to undermine solidarity amongst workers. Tory politicians and writers, popular newspapers and comics deliberately promoted a virulent new form of 'scientific' racism. Partly because of the growing calls for Home Rule, the Irish were the main target of this campaign, which had some success in generating a popular racism.[82] This combined with the ruling-class strategy of reform and co-option to limit solidarity, fragment working-class organisation and in general to contain aspirations for change in the decades after Chartism. But this was a contested process. The years after the Chartists' defeat were not a 'prolonged period of catatonic withdrawal' amongst workers, as Perry Anderson once described it.[83] The more sophisticated state mechanisms didn't extinguish resistance or completely smother internationalism. Most reforms still had to be forced out of the ruling class, and the resulting struggles led to the maturing of socialist ideas amongst a minority. When the 'Great Victorian Boom' ended, socialists moved to the centre of a revived working-class movement.

Struggles continued even in the boom years. A battle by London building workers for a 9-hour day led to the formation of the London Trades Council in 1860 and the launch of a new radical paper, *The Behive*, the next year. The re-emerging movement responded positively to the struggle for unification in Italy and supported the Northern states in the American Civil War, despite the fact that the war decimated cotton production in Britain. The welcoming of Italian Independence leader Garibaldi in 1864 was so big that it took him 6 hours to travel from Nine Elms to St James. The mass celebration, dominated by workers and backed by numerous trade unions, rattled the government so much they cut short Garibaldi's visit. The Working Men's Garibaldi Committee called a protest meeting at Primrose Hill which was violently broken up by police.[84]

These developments led to the launch of the First International in London and Marx's involvement with it. The International initiated the campaign for the 8-hour day which would become the rallying point for a new wave of working-class struggle in the 1880s. It helped to strengthen working-class participation in a number of international campaigns including, crucially, helping sustain a current of English working-class support for Irish Independence. When members of the Fenian Brotherhood were sentenced to execution for killing a police officer in Manchester in 1867, the International led a campaign which culminated in a solidarity meeting of 20,000–25,000 in Clerkenwell Green petitioning for a stay of execution.[85]

The International also supported the revived campaign for universal male suffrage. Limited electoral reform had been proposed by some radical and liberal politicians in the 1860s. Gladstone brought a very mild reform bill to parliament in 1866 which aimed to enfranchise 200,000 more people in the towns. He argued this was necessary to strengthen government, as he had discovered that 'the strength of the modern state lies in its representative system'.[86] He stressed, however, that the Bill would 'not give the absolute majority to the working classes'. Rather than a decisive move towards universal suffrage, it was to be seen more as a reward to a small number of better-off workers for good behaviour, 'a tribute to the working classes' admirable performance at least of their duties towards their superiors', in Gladstone's own words.[87] Once again, fear of insurgency was haunting the reformers. The Radical leader and leading industrialist John Bright warned parliament, 'if you reject the Bill, you will find some accident happening when you will have something more to do than you are asked to do tonight under threats – it may be under the infliction of violence'.[88]

In a letter to Engels, Karl Marx fumed at Bright's hypocrisy, pointing out that he had spoken passionately *against* a Bill designed to limit the working day to 10 hours just the previous year. Bright's double standards encapsulated the more advanced thinking of the bourgeoisie. Bright and his reforming colleagues understood that parliamentary democracy could have the effect of separating workers' economic and political demands, in the process weakening both. The logic was spelt out further by another radical liberal MP, J.T. Hibbert, a partner in an Oldham manufacturing company where trade unions had been suppressed. He argued that working-class MPs were unlikely to bring disputes between bosses and workers into parliament. These, he said, 'were private questions' and 'must be fought outside the House between capital and labour, and not by political discussion'. Widening purely political representation to some working people could have the effect of defusing industrial conflict by de-politicising economic questions and ensuring they were resolved privately behind the factory gates.[89]

Despite this it was mass agitation, particularly by the working-class movement, that drove the new Reform Bill through. Popular pressure also transformed the nature of the legislation. Gladstone's first Bill was narrowly passed by parliament in April 1866 but by June it had foundered as a result of the defeat of an obscure government amendment. The Liberal government died with the reform initiative. No one in parliament seemed to be that concerned.

The mood outside parliament was different. Once the parliamentary initiative had stalled, demands for universal suffrage regained a mass hearing. In July 1866, there were almost daily rallies in Trafalgar Square culminating in a national demonstration planned for 22 July in Hyde Park. This time the growing trade union movement was central to the campaign. The authorities were alarmed. There was no barrier between the park and the centres of political power, as there had been when the Chartists gathered in Kennington, south of the river. With the agreement of the Tory Home Secretary Spencer Walpole, the chief of police decided to ban the demonstration.

Nervous about breaking the law, the middle-class leaders of the Reform League organising the demonstration hit on the compromise of assembling at Marble Arch and marching to Trafalgar Square. The demonstration turned out to be much bigger than expected and many of the protestors refused to move, demanding to be let into Hyde Park. A 3-day long battle with the police followed. Home Secretary Walpole grew increasingly nervous and agreed to meet with a deputation of League leaders. The Tory Prime Minister, Disraeli, started working on some reform proposals. The initial proposals were so weak that they actually boosted the movement. Once again, the authorities banned a demonstration that had been planned for Hyde Park for 6 May 1867. This time the Reform League announced plans to defy the ban. At first the government approached the demonstration as it had the Chartists' Kennington rally. Troops of Hussars and thousands of special constables were prepared. Woolwich Arsenal was ordered to turn out thousands of extra stakes and pikes. But on the day, the government backed off. There were simply too many people arriving from too many directions, too many meetings planned and too much general support in the population for a confrontation to be considered.

The newspapers were apoplectic. They abused the Reform League leaders for fomenting chaos and Walpole for caving in. But the logic of the situation was clear. On 20 May 1867, exactly 2 weeks after the demonstration, Disraeli allowed the Reform Bill to be rewritten in a way that quadrupled the number of workers enfranchised by giving the vote to a million more people. There was strong opposition in the Commons and in the Tory cabinet to this and other changes, but two arguments carried the day. One was Disraeli's insistence that only significant reform would be enough to head off revolt. The other was Lord Balfour's argument that the only political options available in the new parliament would be those that respected what he called 'the foundations of society', by which he meant the maintenance of private property. Under massive pressure from below, and against great internal resistance, the ruling class made just enough concessions to put off universal suffrage for decades.

Roads not taken

Instability returned in the second half of the 1880s when a series of unemployment riots rocked the country. The riots helped to inspire a huge wave of strikes by workers in largely non-unionised industries demanding better pay and union recognition. Britain had been hit by an economic crisis in 1875 which had triggered a decline in foreign investment, a fall in land prices, industrial stagnation and growing unemployment. Its monopoly control of the colonies was under challenge from Germany and the USA. The crisis had coincided with rapid technological change concentrating growing workforces in early mass consumer industries, the gas industry and the expansion of the docks.

Amongst the leaders of the new unionism were a number of talented socialists who had emerged through the Social Democratic Federation, Britain's first Marxist political organisation. Female match workers in East London walked out in response to a leaflet written by socialist agitator Annie Besant and won a major victory which was rapturously received across East London. Their success gave confidence to East London gas workers to win the 8-hour day under the leadership of socialists Will Thorne, John Burns and Eleanor Marx. The new unionism peaked in 1889 when tens of thousands of London dock workers struck and brought around 50 other workplaces out in a movement which came close to a London-wide general strike. The strikes were militant and political. Under Eleanor Marx's influence, the Gas and General Workers Union adopted a policy of equal pay for men's and women's work as early as 1890. These huge struggles, which Will Thorne later described as 'the culmination of long years of Socialist propaganda', had a transformative effect on working people.[90] Engels wrote movingly of the impact of the dock strike in particular:

> Hitherto the East End was bogged down in passive poverty. Lack of resistance on the part of those broken by starvation, of those who had given up all hope was its salient feature... this motley crowd thrown together by chance and changing daily in composition has managed to unite 40,000-strong, to maintain discipline and to strike fear into the hearts of the mighty dock companies. How glad I am to have lived to see this day![91]

The strike wave subsided before it was able to force a new direction in working-class politics. Partly this was a result of repression. The ruling class fought back with organised scabbing and lockouts. The fact that the economy started to pick up again in 1889 also helped to head off a class-wide generalisation of the struggle. But there were also political issues. Despite the vital role played by individual socialists, the Social Democratic Federation as an organisation was dismissive of strike action. It argued that fighting for increased wages was a distraction from the struggle against the wages system. The result was that the socialist strike leaders were alienated from the political organisation in which they had developed. As the labour historian A.L. Morton argues, this reinforced the separation between politics and economics in new ways:

> The 'socialists', the theoretically advanced minority, remained a sect, the mass movement was abandoned to the leadership of all kinds of careerists. Moreover, some of the most militant trade union leaders, Burns and Thorne for example, soon became infected with the opportunism prevailing among the older officials with whom they came into contact. Burns had the distinction of being the first trade union leader to sit in

a Liberal Cabinet. There was never in England that fusion of theory and practice out of which alone right action can grow, and both sides of the movement had to pay dearly for its absence.[92]

The century ended with the first steps towards the foundation of the Labour Party.

A number of key working-class activists had turned to electoral politics as new unionism declined, forming the Independent Labour Party (ILP) in 1893. After more industrial defeats, the ILP's membership fell and its performance in the 1895 elections was poor. The Labour Representation Committee (LRC), the forerunner of the Labour Party, was formed at a conference in London on 27 February 1900. The momentum for the conference was generated by a new round of successful attacks by the employers. Full trade union support for the LRC came only in 1901 following a punitive decision by the courts against Welsh rail strikers known as the Taff Vale judgment. People turned towards a parliamentary project not out of confidence but out of industrial defeat. Responding to employers' victories over engineers and railwaymen, Keir Hardie's paper, the *Labour Leader*, commented:

> Failure. And yet in the end it may turn out that the lesson was worth the cost... it would be more in accordance with the traditional principles of English politics and common sense if the battle was transferred from the poverty stricken homes of the workers to the floor of the house of commons.[93]

The consolidation of the party in the first decade of the twentieth century was a breakthrough, the final victory of the idea of independent working-class political organisation. Though it wasn't until 1924 that it first formed a government, British politics would never be the same again. The party was however very much marked by the circumstances of its birth. Its origins in the wider movement's defeat meant that the party was dominated by the rapidly growing trade union bureaucracy rather than by mobilised or militant workers. It meant that it was an extreme expression of the tendency to separate politics and economics, and its version of politics involved a deep-seated respect for the state and Hardie's 'traditional principles'. Right up until the General Election of 1906, the party was operating a secret electoral pact with the Liberals. While it finally broke organisationally with liberalism, in many ways it took over the mantle of the social liberalism that had emerged towards the end of the nineteenth century. It relied on many liberal ideas for its programme, including an absolute commitment to gradual change from above and the downplaying of any notions of class struggle. The more right-wing leaders like Ramsay MacDonald believed that Labour's role should be to ensure the smooth development of society through the mutual respect of the classes. Those on the Left, like Hardie, were adamant socialists, but they too championed piecemeal reform, appeared confident in the inevitability of progress and elided socialism with the state. All were convinced, in the words of the middle-class Fabians who provided much of the party's early intellectual guidance, that 'Parliament, with all its faults, has always governed in the interest of the class to which the majority of its members belonged... And it will govern in the interests of the people when the majority is selected from the wage-earning class.'[94]

Chapter Four

Three Crises

One of the faults of the system... is that men, when they accept office, are expected immediately to change their attitude towards the great public questions.[95]
George Lansbury MP

Britain's twentieth-century social history is more contested than is often allowed for. The period before the Thatcher government is regularly presented as one of a progressive emergence of a welfare consensus, accelerated by the experience of war and the misery of the Great Depression. In reality, change was hard won and bitterly resisted, and the struggle for it helped to generate a series of political crises. These periods of crisis, after the First World War, after the Second World War and in the mid-1970s, had similarities. They were moments of uncertainty and division in the ruling class. Two were clearly triggered by the experience of modern, total war. Popular discontent was a contributing factor in all three, and militant class struggle a constituent cause of the two most serious crises. In each case, state institutions worked hard to try and maintain the status quo. Facing a government with a more radical programme at a time of economic decline and social danger, the state moved more energetically against the Wilson and Callaghan governments in the 1970s than it had against previous Labour administrations. But all three experiences provide clear evidence of various wings of the state colluding in the job of limiting change and maintaining control by whatever means they felt were necessary. They also show the decisive importance of the nature of the political approach taken by those seeking to make change happen.

The state was, in fact, facing crisis before the First World

War. Militant strikes by seafarers and dockers in 1909 marked the beginning of the most serious workers' insurgency since the Chartists. Ireland was in turmoil. British rule was threatened by mass agitation in Ireland itself, and the Liberal government needed the support of the Irish Home Rule Party to survive. After the defeat of a massive Irish strike wave, Tory politicians backed the new 100,000-strong Ulster Volunteer Force to crush the movement. In April 1914, the government ordered troops based in Dublin to head north to challenge them. The army refused, revealing its independence from government. All this combined with the suffragettes' confrontational campaign for votes for women to create something close to panic in ruling-class circles.

There was, too, an underlying anxiety that Britain was losing its leading edge in manufacturing and trade. By 1913, both Germany and the USA had outstripped Britain in the production of iron and steel and the new chemical and electronics industries. The British war against the Boer settlers in South Africa was part of an increasingly interventionist imperial policy. But a series of defeats at the hands of the Boers led to calls for a programme of national reconstruction spearheaded by a more active state. It was Lloyd George's Liberal Party rather than the Labour group of MPs that set the pace with a series of populist reforms including insurance, health schemes and land reforms. This caused a constitutional crisis. After the House of Lords vetoed the government's 1909 budget, Lloyd George was forced to confront the power of the Lords by removing its veto over legislation.

Lloyd George's social liberalism was not capable of containing the crisis. Many of the leaders of the strikes defined themselves as syndicalists, seeing strikes as a vehicle for wider social change. Action spread to the railways, led to the formation of a 'Triple Alliance' between the transport workers, miners and railway workers, and threatened a general strike. It was the outbreak of war that headed off confrontation, as the bulk of the Left and the labour movement in Britain and around the world supported their governments' war efforts. The war accelerated moves towards state intervention. Reluctantly, the ruling class had to face the fact that market mechanisms are useless in the emergency conditions of mechanised warfare. In Eric Hobsbawm's words, 'by 1919, the government had taken over the running of several industries, controlled others by requisitioning or licensing, organised its own bulk purchases abroad, restricted capital expenditure and foreign trade, fixed prices and controlled the distribution of consumer goods'.[96] But despite government promises that the men who won the war would win the peace, interventionism was largely abandoned after the war. The practicality of state involvement had been proved, but by 1922 most of the machinery of government control of industry was broken up.[97]

1919-1926

The British state came closest to losing control in the 2 years after the First World War. Despite the pre-war reforms and a big extension of the franchise in 1918, the hellish experience of the war and the demands for sacrifice at home and abroad had combined with the experience of wartime big government to renew demands for change. A wave of revolutionary action across Europe increased tension. Trade union militancy had returned on a grand scale. It was led by engineers but threatened to spread as the war ended and all three unions in the Triple Alliance registered pay demands. By early 1919, cabinet records show that the government was dealing with little other than strikes. Its meeting of 31 January, for example, discussed strikes in Belfast and Glasgow, the demands of the miners, the 'Railway Situation' in which the men were 'in some measure out of hand', and a coming tube strike. The Glasgow engineers' strike for a 40-hour week was particularly alarming. The secretary of state for Scotland feared that 'it was a misnomer to call the situation a strike – it was a Bolshevist rising'.[98]

The Glasgow strike was indeed impressive. Despite the fact that the engineers who led it failed to get official support from most of the other unions, 40,000 came out on the first day and the strike spread quickly at rank and file level to involve 100,000. The strike radicalised the whole city. One participant claimed, 'we have had as many as five thousand females forming one of our massed pickets'.[99] By the third day of the strike, all factories were closed. Belfast had come out a few days earlier on an unofficial general strike for the 44-hour week and there the city was brought to a standstill. Workers in the two cities were in daily communication and a telegram to the cabinet claimed that in Belfast, 'the workmen have formed a "Soviet" Committee'.[100] Around the same time, The Clyde Workers' Committee's newspaper declared: 'We "British Bolsheviks" have the Russian precedent to guide us, we believe that in the critical hours of our own revolution, our rallying cry will be: "All Power to the Workers Committees"'.[101]

Strike action in the mines and on the railways was creating pressure on the union leadership to organise national action. But what made the situation particularly threatening was the fact that industrial unrest coincided with militant action in the police force and the army. Police strikes had begun in the late summer of 1918, demanding better pay and union recognition. Alarmingly, when Prime Minister Lloyd George sat down to meet the president of the newly formed National Union of Police and Prison Officers, he was informed that the soldiers who had been brought into replace the striking police had announced that they would refuse to move against them.[102]

Mutinies in the army began early the next year after notices were posted at Folkestone barracks that 2,000 men were to embark to France to join the campaign against the new Soviet regime in Russia. Following a mass meeting, columns of soldiers marched through the town chanting 'are we going to France? No! Are we going home? Yes!'[103] There were 10,000 soldiers involved by the time the troops reached the town hall. A soldiers' union was set up and disturbances spread rapidly through the garrisons of hundreds of thousands of returned troops across southern England and beyond. Days later, 1,500 troops from Park Royal in north-west London marched on Downing Street, demanding to speak to the Prime Minister.

The soldiers were infuriated by the slow pace of demobilisation, sick of terrible conditions and bitterly opposed to plans to send reinforcements to the Russian front. By 19 January, even Winston Churchill, the main champion of war with Russia, was forced to admit that if there was any further delay in demobilisation, the army would be a 'demoralised and angry mob'. Discipline was breaking down even faster in the army abroad. There were mutinies across France and rumours from the Russian front that some British soldiers had set up a soldiers' soviet.[104] The government had had no choice but to give in to the soldiers. They had done the same with the police strikes the previous year, granting a bigger pay rise than the union had demanded.[105] But they were still concerned about the reliability of both forces.

Fearing the development of a revolutionary mood, the ruling class responded to the wider unrest with a carefully calibrated combination of force, manoeuvre and tactical retreat. They were sensitive both to the objective balance of forces and the political strengths and weaknesses of the movement. Relatively isolated, the Glasgow strikes could be smashed. A huge demonstration in George Square on 31 January was viciously broken up by the police. The next day hundreds of soldiers – mainly raw recruits – were sent from England to turn Glasgow into an armed camp. The rank and file leaders of the strikes were arrested and imprisoned. This allowed the national trade union leaders to suspend both the Belfast and the Glasgow strike committees.

The strikes were over by mid-February.

The Triple Alliance was another matter. Coal, the railways and other transport networks were essential to the day to day running of the country, and the alliance of national unions had the power to bring the country to a standstill. To make matters worse, the leaders of the miners and the transport workers, Robert Smillie and Robert Williams, were high-profile left-wingers. The ruling class adopted a twin track approach. On the one hand, they promised concessions to the unions to buy them off and divide them, on the other hand they threatened more repression. In reality, this last gesture was a bluff. Given the insubordination in the army and the police force, a policy of confrontation with mass strike action was hopeless. But it worked as psychology, at least with the trade union leaders. Robert Smillie later explained his thinking to the TUC: 'If there is a strike they will use the soldiers,' he said, 'my people will be shot down. Anything rather than that.'[106]

In the run up to the strike threatened by the Triple Alliance, rail workers and miners were offered pay rises and a shorter working week. Miners were promised an 'effective voice in the direction of the mines'.[107] Labour politicians did their best to persuade them against strike action, apparently with some effect.[108] But the attitude of the trade union leaders was the decisive factor in heading off confrontation. Lloyd George understood the leaders' instinct for compromise and negotiation and exploited it to the full. A report of his comments in a meeting with the leaders of the Triple Alliance and Robert Smillie's reaction are so telling they deserve quoting at length:

'Gentlemen, you have fashioned, in the Triple Alliance of the unions represented by you, a most powerful instrument. I feel bound to tell you that in our opinion we are at your mercy. The army is disaffected and cannot be relied upon. Trouble has occurred already in a number of camps. We have just emerged from a great war and the people are eager for the reward of their sacrifice, and we are in no position to satisfy them. In these circumstances, if you carry out your threat and strike, then you will defeat us. But if you do so, have you weighed the consequences? The strike will be in defiance of the Government of this country and by its very success will precipitate a constitutional crisis of the first importance. For, if a force arises in the State that is stronger than the State itself, then it must be ready to take on the functions of the State itself, or withdraw and accept the authority of the State. Gentlemen, have you considered, and if you have, are you ready?' 'From that moment on,' said Robert Smillie, 'we were beaten and we knew we were.'[109]

The strike was called off, but while the revolutionary mood receded in the following months, key aspects of the crisis were unresolved. In May 1920, East London dockers prevented munitions being sent to Poland to help fight the Bolsheviks on the *Jolly George*. When Lloyd George announced a plan to send troops to Poland to fight the Russians, the TUC and the Labour Party organised a Council of Action and threatened a general strike. Local Councils of Action quickly spread across the country and in many places became the hub of working-class organisation.[110]

The government quietly dropped its war plans. Early the following year, the government announced it was going to hand the coal mines back to their pre-war private owners. The terms of the deal included an end to national negotiations and massive wage cuts. The Miners' Federation refused the deal and on 1 April the government declared a state of emergency. A week later, the Triple Alliance called for a national strike. Despite massive enthusiasm for action amongst the rank and file, once again the union leaders pulled back from the brink, this time calling off action the day before the planned strike.

The day of the cancelled action became known as 'Black Friday'. The retreat was a stunning blow to the whole labour movement and in the words of one historian, 'a failure of courage'. It was also one more indication of the preference of union leaders for compromise over confrontation.[111]

In the wake of this defeat, the initiative in the labour movement passed to the Labour Party. Labour was handed office for the first time in 1924 in a hung parliament. The party's strategy was decided privately and secretly at a meeting at the house of the Fabian intellectual Sidney Webb, attended only by party leader Ramsay MacDonald's inner circle. They agreed that the priority was to prove that Labour would put the national interest first and was capable of taming its 'wild men' of the Left. Much to the annoyance of the TUC, Labour's National Executive Committee and many of its activists, the government kept trade union leaders at arm's length in order to prove its 'national' character, failed to revoke anti-labour laws and threatened to use troops against strikers.[112] There were some reforms, including John Wheatley's Housing Act, which cleared the way for a significant increase in council housing, but Labour's first ever budget set the tone. Chancellor Phillip Snowden reduced duties on some essentials, abolished some protective tariffs and cut corporation tax. This was a budget that he proudly claimed was 'vindictive against no class and no interest'. As he recalled, its reception 'was everything I could have desired. It relieved the feelings of the rich, who had feared that there might be drastic impositions on their class.'[113]

Despite the government's moderation and its efforts to distance itself from the Left, after a few months it was met by a vicious campaign of red-baiting in parliament. The Liberals and the Tories harassed Labour over its policy of recognising the Russian Soviet government and, in the summer, they went on the attack over the government's decision not to prosecute the editor of a communist newspaper who had called for troops to refuse to turn their guns on fellow workers. MacDonald chose to make the issue a matter of confidence and lost the vote. The election that followed was dominated by the appearance in the *Daily Mail* of a letter claiming to be from the Comintern president Zinoviev, addressed to the British Communist Party, calling for a strengthening of the Russian treaties as a means of extending 'the propaganda ideas of Leninism in England and the Colonies'.[114] The red scare and the 'Zinoviev Letter' didn't damage Labour's polling, which actually went up by a million votes. It did, however, help to frighten many Liberal supporters into voting for the Conservatives, who won the October 1924 election decisively.

Labour's lacklustre performance in office and its election defeat reignited the mood for industrial resistance. In July 1925, a special conference of trade union executives backed the General Council of the TUC's calls for industrial action to defend the miners against a new round of wage cuts. At the last minute, the government backed off from plans to cut its coal subsidy. But the cuts were only postponed till the report of a government commission on the future of mining was delivered on 1 May 1926. In the months that followed, the state made preparations for a decisive showdown with the unions. The Organisation for the Maintenance of Supplies was formed by a number of retired diplomats and military officers in case of a general strike. It self-presented as neutral and independent but had the blessing of the Home Secretary and the backing of British fascists. By the eve of the General Strike, when it was handed over to the government, it had recruited around 100,000 volunteers to maintain public services, and deal with disorder. Meanwhile the government had already organised its own supply and transport service. The leaders of the Labour movement did nothing to prepare. Right up until the start of the strike on 3 May 1926, the priority of the General Council of the TUC was to head off action through a negotiated settlement, even if necessary one that the miners would find unacceptable. In the end, the government forced the strike on the TUC by issuing an impossible ultimatum.

The government handled the strike with skill. Far from idling around playing football with the strikers, as has sometimes been suggested, the police and the volunteer constables repeatedly attacked pickets and strike meetings. Troops and armoured cars were used to intimidate strikers and protect strike breakers. An American observer noted: 'There were enough armaments in the London docks to kill every living thing in every street in the neighbourhood of the mills.'[115] Chancellor of the Exchequer Winston Churchill led the hawks in government pushing to treat the strike as a revolutionary challenge to constitutional government. The official communique published on 8 May claimed, 'an organised attempt is being made to starve the people and wreck the state'.[116] Prime Minister Baldwin, equally convinced of the necessity of a crushing victory but concerned about keeping the wider public on board, was less antagonistic in public. In general, the establishment presented the strike as illegal and illegitimate. The BBC, while resisting Churchill's demands that it should be commandeered, famously took the view that as it was 'for the people and that the government is for the people, it follows that the BBC must be for the government in this crisis too'.[117]

Despite the intimidation and propaganda, the rank and file of the labour movement was enthusiastic and determined. The turnout for the strike and the self-organisation and militancy of the strikers increased daily. In most places the trades councils became dynamic organising centres of a more and more active strike. According to research done at the time, 'with very few exceptions indeed, the Councils displayed energy and initiative to an extent that astonished all who had known them in the proceeding period'.[118] The surge of working-class initiative was so effective that after a few days, in some areas, strike committees were sharing control of towns and cities with the authorities.[119] The leaderships of the TUC and the Labour Party, on the other hand, were looking for the quickest possible way out of a situation they found frankly threatening. Ramsay MacDonald was in 'continual touch with the government side... regarding settlement of the strike'.[120] A week after the strike began, the General Council of the TUC was demanding that the miners accept a new but still humiliating offer. The miners' leaders refused, but despite this and the deepening of the strike action, the General Council went to Downing Street the next day offering Prime Minister Baldwin their unconditional surrender.

The post-war crisis was contained. The state responded to the greatest threat it faced any time in the twentieth century with skill and sophistication.[121] It deployed force at key moments, it made concessions to workers' demands and promised reforms. It ensured that the media was on message, used propaganda to try and isolate the strikers from wider society and beefed up bureaucratic bargaining structures to incorporate trade unions further into state structures. But the crisis led to profound changes in the nature of the state. The liberal bloc, which had played such an important role in developing capitalism, fractured. The increasing weight of organised workers in society meant that the project of state-led reform was more and more associated with Labour. The convergence of interests between big capitalists, bankers and landowners was reflected in the emergence of the Tory Party as the main party of the ruling class. As a result, the period saw the arrival of Labour as a potential party of government. And despite defeats for workers, the sheer scale of working-class mobilisation helped to lay the basis for the emergence of a new social settlement after the Second World War. But the crisis also showed the contingent nature of capitalist rule at certain moments of danger. It showed that even in an 'advanced' capitalist society, action by working people can begin to undermine the power of the state. At critical points in these years it was the approach of the majority of the leaders of trade unions, backed by the Labour leaders, that guaranteed state survival. Committed to constitutional change and fearful of losing control, the majority of them preferred setback – and even defeat – to a challenge to the structures of the state.

1945-1951

Clement Attlee's Labour government marked the high point of state-led change in Britain. It nationalised important parts of industry, massively expanded welfare, instituted a state education system and, of course, founded the National Health Service. Labour's 1945 landslide victory against Winston Churchill was a political upset, but many commentators had already noted a radical mood generated by the war and the Great Depression. Terrible sacrifices had been made and the war had shown once again that central planning could work. In the hardest years of the war, George Orwell noted a strong desire for more equality, and a feeling that socialist planning was necessary to win the war and create a decent society afterwards.[122] Labour Party intellectual Harold Laski agreed, arguing in 1943 that people:

> will not endure, after victory, the persistence of mass unemployment... they will not accept the emergence of distressed areas... they will not submit, at least peacefully to any rebuilding of Britain which allows the ground landlord and the speculative builder to profiteer out of the sufferings of Coventry and Plymouth, East London and Merseyside.[123]

More thoughtful members of the ruling class also sensed the need for change. Two years before the election, Tory reformer Quintin Hogg had remarked, 'if you do not give the people social reforms they will give you revolution'. Lord Hinchingbrooke, the chair of Hogg's Tory reform group, expressed unease about the experience of the 1930s, claiming, 'true conservative opinion is horrified at the damage done to this country since the last war by "individualist" business-men, financiers and speculators'.[124] The 1942 Beveridge Report, written by liberal reformer Sir William Beveridge, outlined a plan for a significant expansion of the welfare state, including enhanced social security, pensions and a comprehensive national service. A total of 635,000 copies were sold and polls showed 86 per cent wanted it implemented, as against 6 per cent who opposed. Amongst the national press, only the *Daily Telegraph* campaigned against it.[125]

The embrace of the state by parts of the establishment wasn't only a response to the radicalising of public opinion. In the 1930s, state involvement in the economy had become the norm internationally and an increasing number of politicians were converts to state demand management policies proposed by John Maynard Keynes. Their ideas appeared to be vindicated by the experience of the war. By 1941, about 49 per cent of the total working population was working for the government in one way or another and the war had ended 2 decades of economic decline.[126] At a time when Britain was falling behind internationally, there seemed little alternative to using the state to modernise the economy. For all these reasons, most of Labour's nationalisations went through parliament quite easily. The first measure, the nationalisation of the Bank of England, was even supported by Winston Churchill.[127] The establishment of the National Coal Board was not much more controversial. Many Tory backbenchers deeply resented the changes taking place, but no leading Tory openly opposed it and the Mining Association withdrew its opposition to nationalisation 'because of the result of the general election'. As one historian of the period comments:

> This lamb-like utterance... was not unconnected with the fact that the antiquated machinery of industry had been worked to its limit during the war and now needed drastic renewal, that

manpower would soon be scarce enough to win concessions, and that oil looked like undercutting the monopoly value of coal. It was not a bad time to sell out.[128]

Labour's first 2 years were impressive. Following on from the mines, electricity, gas, civil aviation, cable and wireless, railways and much road haulage were nationalised. Powers were introduced to allow trade and industry departments to redistribute and reorganise elements of industry. Beveridge's social security and national insurance plans were enacted, creating a comprehensive safety net for the unemployed and sick. The government's greatest achievement was the NHS. Aneuran Bevan and his colleagues faced down many of the objections from doctors and consultants to his project and the NHS created an extraordinarily successful system that largely excluded market pressures from public healthcare.[129] These measures didn't just bring dramatic material improvements to the lives of working people, they also increased democratic control over society. At least theoretically, by the 1950s, elected governments were in control of around 20 per cent of the economy. Health and social welfare were now fully accepted as issues of public policy. Against a background of a broadly expanding economy, some of the popular aspirations for change had been met, and Labour was rewarded with continued support from working people.

What the government didn't do was fulfil the wartime hopes of Laski and others that the powers of the economic oligarchy would be decisively pushed back, opening a path to a more collective, democratic control of the economy. The new boards that were set up to run nationalised industries were dominated by elite bureaucrats and captains of industry. The head of the new Coal Board, for example, had been involved in one of the big private coal companies and many of the managers the Board employed were recruited directly from the previous managements. Worker involvement in running the new enterprises was ruled out as impractical by the government.[130]

Equally tellingly, the government paid out huge sums in compensation to the owners of industries that were to be nationalised. The sums involved were vast enough to have a significant impact on the direction of the economy and the nature of the post-war society. In the words of Paul Foot:

> The coal-owners for instance, responsible for at least a century of exploitation, starvation and eviction in mining areas, picked up £164 million in Government stock (equivalent in 2002 to £2.5 billion). This massive pay-out, repeated in the proposals for electricity, gas, cables and aviation, tipped the balance of class forces in favour of the rich. More than any other Government measure, the compensation largesse ensured that the rich and the super-rich kept their distance from the poor during the period of the Labour government. Indeed, some argued that the payment of such huge sums in compensation for clapped-out old stock and vulnerable industries diverted the resources of the rich into more profitable areas than they would otherwise have occupied.[131]

As Harold Wilson noted, there was little theoretical consideration in the Labour Party of how the government should relate to private industry and this 'vacuum in Socialist thought' extended to the nature of state institutions.[132] In fact, the main change to state institutions was the dismantling of many of the agencies that had been involved in running the war time economy. In 1944, the coalition government had agreed to keep the Treasury at the centre of economic planning and management, a decision that went unquestioned by the incoming Labour government. On taking office, Attlee centralised the government by increasing his own control over the cabinet.[133] But despite the huge planned increase in state responsibilities, there was no attempt to restructure the civil service and certainly no democratisation of the state. Constitutional arrangements were untouched and the House of Lords was left intact.

In the civil service itself there was active and conscious opposition to change. In May 1946, two meetings of the permanent secretaries rejected the idea of any overhaul of the civil service to deal with the new functions of the state. New roles were simply grafted on to existing institutions. This was not traditionalism for its own sake; such 'archaism' was part of a strategy to block state democratisation. Any major restructuring would have meant the possibility of representatives of new social forces gaining a foothold in state institutions. This was to be avoided at all costs. In the words of one sociologist, 'it would have required a more radical political explosion than that registered in the ballot boxes of 1945 to have dislodged key participants in the British state'.[134]

The government's approach to industry was based on the assumption of shared national interests in modernisation. When it strayed beyond that, it encountered strong resistance. The most contested nationalisation was that of the iron and steel industry, which was considered both fairly profitable and efficient. In Attlee's words, 'of all our nationalisation programmes, only iron and steel aroused much feeling, perhaps because profits were greater here than elsewhere'.[135] This was an understatement. The owners fought iron and steel nationalisation relentlessly. They refused to take part in negotiations and waged a propaganda campaign in the country against what they called 'confiscation'. Privately, Attlee lobbied for a government retreat, but the cabinet insisted on full nationalisation. Despite this, the Bill was watered down and postponed until after the 1950 election. The government's attempt to set up development councils as a way of co-ordinating industry also failed in the teeth of growing resistance from industry. Harold Wilson was shocked by the employers' opposition to what appeared to be a relatively anodyne policy.[136] The truth was that reliance on voluntary policies meant retreat in the face of opposition.

Respect for the status quo was most obvious in foreign policy. Despite talk of a socialist foreign policy in opposition, on the day after the election results, the new Foreign Secretary, Ernest Bevin, announced, 'British foreign policy will not be altered in any way under a Labour government.'[137] In the first years after the Second World War, Britain spent a higher proportion of GNP on defence than any other Western nation. It tried to hold on to empire wherever possible. It sent troops to help the French crush an uprising in Indo-China and it worked hard to develop the best possible relations with the Nationalist government in South Africa as it established apartheid. In 1949, the government pushed through legislation to make the gerrymandered Protestant state of the six counties permanent, despite a sizeable rebellion amongst MPs. Labour's Indian policy is often cited as an example of enlightened attitudes, but it was actually an unavoidable reaction to an Indian insurgency. Lord Ismay, who was on the government's team overseeing the transfer of power, later made the situation clear: 'India in March, 1947, was a ship on fire in mid-ocean with ammunition in the hold. By then it was a question of putting out the fire before it reached the ammunition. There was, in fact, no option but to do what we did.'[138]

The key innovation in Labour's foreign policy was the 'special relationship' with the USA. It was obvious Britain was not going to be able to sustain its position as the main world power, but by tying its interests to those of its successor in that role, it hoped to maintain a military presence in key areas, including parts of the Middle East and South East Asia, and benefit from being the USA's most loyal ally. Ernest Bevin helped launch NATO partly in order to secure Britain's position as the USA's indispensable ally in Europe. The government also sent significant forces to support the USA in its war in Korea. Meanwhile, to avoid complete subservience to the USA, Attlee and Bevin, without reference to the American government, the British parliament or even the cabinet, committed millions of pounds to developing a secret British nuclear arms programme.

The failure to challenge the priorities of the establishment and the state had consequences for every aspect of policy. It meant, for one thing, that the government took an entirely conventional attitude to organised labour. No attempt was made to open up government to working people. Support from the trade union leaders helped keep strikes to a minimum in the first years of the administration, but by the end of the 1940s, when a worsening economy led to increased strike action, the government reacted aggressively. In May 1947, Aneuran Bevan called for legal moves against striking dockworkers and later he used troops to transport people to work during a Birmingham bus workers' strike. In total, between 1945 and 1951, the army was ordered to cross picket lines and do strikers' jobs 18 times.[139] It meant, too, that when confronted with economic problems, the government reached for traditional solutions.[140] Facing a financial crisis in 1947, the government introduced a programme of cuts in exchange for a big loan from the US government. Despite this, sterling was sold on a huge scale, causing a huge drain on the reserves. A similar speculative crisis 2 years later led the government to devalue the pound. Under pressure from the papers and big business, the government scrapped economic controls on business and cut the food rations that had done so much to improve workers' standards of living. In October 1949, the cabinet announced a further package of cuts worth £280 million.[141]

The Attlee government achieved a new settlement which shaped the British state for decades. The more active state with a responsibility for basic welfare that had been tentatively suggested by the nineteenth-century Liberals had been enacted by Labour. Working people had forced the state to recognise their existence and their demands, even if it didn't fulfil them.

One result was that the Liberals were marginalised as Labour and the Tories became the two great parties of office. Subsequent governments of both parties had to continue to relate to working-class aspirations. But the post-war government also settled in practice the question of what kind of social system the Labour Party stood for. While Labour had always embraced the idea of gradual, evolutionary change through parliament, it had also often used the language of socialism. The failure of its first two governments in 1924 and 1929-31 to transform society could be explained by the fact that they had both been minority administrations. For all its great achievements, the Attlee government firmly positioned Labour as a party of social democracy and a mixed economy, committed not to transforming the system, but to trying to make capitalism work better for everyone.

1974-79

The Wilson Labour government that took office in 1974 appeared at first to challenge the idea of Labour as a moderate social democratic party. It swept in on a powerful wave of working-class struggle. Two militant miners' strikes had shaken the Tory government and the miners' victorious 1972 strike had ignited action in the docks, engineering and construction. Manchester engineers followed the example of radical students and the Clyde ship workers, and occupied their factories. A series of victories smashed the Tories' incomes policy and forced the government to introduce big subsidies for industry. As a study of the strikes of 1972 explains, victory was infectious:

> As in all extraordinary periods of class struggle, the whole of society was affected. The very public success of some of the big disputes helped to inspire protests that year by other groups. In May a school students' strike in London led to the formation of the National Union of School Students.

Preservation of the Rights of Prisoners was established, and a series of sit-downs in May and June culminated in a prison strike in August. On 1 October rent strikes were launched in over 80 towns and cities. There were also strikes over the Housing Finance Act in Liverpool and Dundee in October and over state pensions in Scunthorpe in November. At the end of October 500 Asian workers at the Mansfield Hosiery Mills in Loughborough went on strike for a large pay rise and an end to discrimination in job opportunities in the factory.[142]

The situation was so serious that Tory Prime Minister Edward Heath felt obliged to go to the country in February 1974, asking the question 'who rules Britain?', by which he meant his government or the unions. He lost. At a time of growing economic crisis, Labour had narrowly won the election on its most radical manifesto ever. Influenced by widespread working-class militancy, the manifesto promised a 'fundamental and irreversible shift in the balance of power in favour of working people and their families', to make 'power in industry genuinely accountable to the workers and the community at large' and to 'socialise existing nationalised industries'.[143] High-profile left-wingers were in key cabinet positions. Tony Benn, who had been moving steadily to the left, was given the job of Secretary of State for Industry. He chose Liverpool socialist MP Eric Heffer as his deputy. Michael Foot, the one survivor of the Attlee government, was made Minister for Employment. Despite being a minority government, Wilson's administration moved quite decisively on taking office. In its first 6 months, it settled with the miners, scrapped a Tory Housing Act, raised welfare payments and increased taxes on the rich. The Left's forward momentum was sustained through a second election, in which Labour won a small overall majority, and into 1975.

With its radical manifesto and against the recent background of workers' militancy, the Wilson government met with much more concerted opposition from the state and big business than Attlee's. Heading up the Department of Industry with a radical agenda, Tony Benn was a particular target of the establishment. Soon after the election, one of the directors of leading engineering firm GKN privately threatened him with an investment strike if his company was not taken off the target list of companies to be nationalised.[144] Benn experienced bare-faced obstruction from civil servants in his department. According to his diaries, his Permanent Secretary, Sir Anthony Part, treated him 'like a consultant psychiatrist would a particularly dangerous patient' and asked him incredulously if he really intended to go ahead with his economic programme. When Benn assured him that he did, Part replied, 'well, I must warn you, in that case, that if you do it, you will be heading for as big a confrontation with industrial management as the last Government had with the trade unions'.[145] Benn was also undermined by members of his own cabinet, including the Prime Minister, who tried to ban him from making speeches. Just a few months after taking office, Benn explained the situation to cabinet colleague Roy Jenkins. 'Look. This is what is really happening,' he said:

All my industrial and regional policy in respect of Europe is being taken away and put under the Foreign Secretary's control. My Green Paper is being blocked by the Treasury, by the Chancellor's minute. My day to day business is now being watched… All my speeches are controlled, and indeed I have been told by the Prime Minister not to speak or broadcast. And as regards appointments, the Prime Minister has said I am not to proceed even by letting it be known there are vacancies. This is the position I am in and do you wonder that, frustrated within Whitehall, I turn outside, where my support is?[146]

Meanwhile, MI5 and a host of other shadowy organisations were working to smear and discredit members of the government, including Harold Wilson himself. Former MI5 officer Peter Wright later claimed that in the run up to the second election of 1974, 'MI5 would arrange for selective details of the intelligence about leading Labour Party figures, especially Wilson, to be leaked to sympathetic pressmen'.[147] Overseas Development Minister Judith Hart was removed from the cabinet by Harold Wilson on the basis of false claims from the security services that she had communist links. Benn felt that he was under surveillance and when he confronted the Home Secretary, Merlyn Rees, with his suspicions that his phone was tapped, Rees told him, 'he couldn't say yes or no'.[148]

The security services were working with a range of extra-parliamentary organisations that had set themselves up to take control of the country in the event of government collapse. In 1974, for example, Colonel Davis Stirling, one of the founders of the Special Air Service, set up GB75, an organisation with the declared intention of a takeover of the government.[149] But the immediate aim was the subversion and disorientation of the Labour government. On the basis of documents presented to him by the security services, Harold Wilson caused a sensation in parliament in May 1974 when he claimed that the IRA was plotting to reduce the whole of Ulster to rubble in a 'scorched earth' combat policy. The plot turned out to be a 2-year old security service fabrication, but Wilson's announcement was applauded by the Right and helped to generate tension across the country.[150]

Despite these plots and provocations, and the planned extension of state intervention in society, neither the government nor the Left in Labour turned their attention to reforming the state. As Paul Hirst has put it, their Keynesian economic programme remained, 'a change of policy – not of the constitution, not the relation of the citizen to the state, and not of the basic forms of property ownership'.[151]

The Left's progress was checked in the summer of 1975 by a referendum on new terms for staying in the European Common Market, the EEC. The Left in Labour – including Tony Benn and six other cabinet members – opposed the deal on the basis that continued membership of the EEC weakened democracy and would make it harder to push through a radical economic programme. The remain side, generously backed and funded by big capitalist interests, won the June 1975 referendum by more than two to one. This victory gave Wilson the confidence to move against the Left in his cabinet. Heffer was sacked and Benn was demoted to Energy Minister, all apparently on the basis of a deal that Wilson had made with the City.[152] The balance of power in the cabinet shifted decisively.

Though parts of business and of the media had been campaigning for Benn's removal from the Department of Industry since his appointment, it wasn't enough for them. Later in the summer, sabotage and subversion shifted to the economic front. The context would have been difficult for any government. An oil price shock and the policy of printing money had generated a record 24.6 per cent inflation level by 1975. Unemployment had reached one million. Investors and currency speculators were using inflation as an excuse to pull out of the British economy. In the summer of 1975, there was a massive run on the pound. On 30 June, so much sterling was sold that the pound fell further than on any other single day in history. With the Left defeated, the option of deepening government control over the economy and introducing currency controls was off the table. Under pressure from the bankers and the international markets, the government ended up imposing wage restraint and seeking IMF loans tied to cuts in public spending on hospitals, schools and on government investment in industry.

Surviving figures on the Left in cabinet were used to sell this policy to the party.

At Labour's conference in the autumn, Michael Foot was

given the job of trying to justify this change of direction. 'We face an economic typhoon of unparalleled ferocity, the worse the world has seen since the 1930s,' he said, and it needed to be faced with 'socialist imagination' and the 'red flame of socialist courage'. He got a standing ovation.[153] But the speech signalled that Labour had shifted to a course diametrically opposed to the one on which it had been elected. It was a course that involved ending a 30-year run of full employment and expanding public services. The following year, Wilson's successor as Prime Minister, James Callaghan, confirmed to conference that the change was permanent and that the Keynesian experiment was over:

> We used to think that you could spend your way out of a recession, and increase employment by cutting taxes and boosting government spending. I will tell you in all candour that that option no longer exists, and that in so far as it ever did exist it only worked on each occasion since the war by injecting a bigger dose of inflation into the economy, followed by a higher level of unemployment.[154]

The union leaderships had no other political strategy than to support a Labour government and for some time they managed to sell this reversal to their members. The result was disastrous for workers. It was so bad that in 1977 an *Observer* economist could write, 'the past twelve months have certainly seen the sharpest fall in the real living standards of Britain's working population in any year for at least a century, including the wars. Indeed, to find a comparable fall, it will be necessary to go back to the eighteenth and early nineteenth centuries.'[155] The trade union leaders' jobs were made easier by the fact that the networks of shop stewards that had led the big struggles of the early 1970s had been partially incorporated by a strategy of industrial co-operation. This often involved them coming off the shop floor, making them more vulnerable to management's business logic. But just as important, the dominant forces of the Left saw the role of the rank and file movement as being to pressure the leadership of the unions rather than acting independently: 'to activate the official leadership of the unions and the TUC, not to replace it,' in the Communist Party's words.[156] As a result, they followed the official line and regarded a Labour government as the only realistic political option.

In the government's fourth year, bitterness exploded in the 'winter of discontent' – a huge strike wave led by public sector workers against cuts and wage restraint. The level of action was remarkable. More strike days were 'lost' in 1979 than in 1972, the high point of the anti-Tory struggles, and services were brought to a standstill around the country.[157] But having reluctantly accepted the logic of the Labour government's retrenchment, the bulk of the Left was in no position to provide a lead for this new round of resistance. Without a political strategy for taking on a Labour government, the movement reached an impasse that couldn't be overcome by the most heroic trade union activism.

In a situation of acute economic crisis, failure to challenge the priorities of the state in the 1970s had much more serious consequences than it had in the post-war government. After a first year of progress, the experience of the Labour governments of the 1970s was dreadful for working people. The cuts introduced were harsher than anything Thatcher managed.[158] Worse still, the government's acceptance of the logic of the free market and the resulting disappointment and disorientation of Labour's base helped lay the basis for what followed: the root and branch implementation of neoliberalism.

Chapter Five

Shock and Awe

Our approach certainly was hit first, hit hard and keep on hitting.[159]
Maurice Saatchi, PR advisor to Margaret Thatcher

Margaret Thatcher famously claimed to be suspicious of the state. Her rhetoric was an updated mix of liberal free-market dogma and Tory traditionalism. The state was once again the enemy and the spirit of liberty was to be found in the markets and the traditional good sense and habits of ordinary people. In the words of Thatcherite think tank Centre for Policy Studies, the aim was to 'limit the role of the state, to encourage enterprise and to enable the institutions of society – such as families and voluntary organisations – to flourish'.[160] As her project evolved, Thatcher gave free-market fatalism a new twist by claiming that the market was the only game in town. 'There is no way in which one can buck the market,' she said, and simply, 'there is no alternative'.[161]

Once again, elite fatalism aimed not only to justify the status quo and demoralise opposition, but to create the conditions for decisive action. The history of the Thatcher years and the neoliberal decades that followed contradicts the conventional view that the state has shrunk, and even the idea common on the Left that it has been 'hollowed out'. State spending actually rose throughout this period.[162] This was partly because neoliberalism increased poverty and successive governments have not been able to cut the welfare bill as much as they hoped. It is partly too because outsourcing has turned out to be an extremely expensive way of delivering services. But it is also the result of two other important things about Thatcher's project. One was that state institutions of all sorts played a central, active and at times brutal part in the rollout of neoliberalism. The other was that the state was significantly re-engineered to perform new functions. Neoliberalism was not a conspiracy nor a coherent plan imposed on society by a clique. It was an evolving set of policies implemented by the dominant sections of the ruling class, often with unforeseen consequences. But remodelling the state has been a priority. In the words of Stephen Gill, one of the neoliberals' main aims has been 'to insulate the commanding heights of economic policy from democratic control or scrutiny and place it in the hands of capital, and primarily financial interests'.[163]

Discussion of the neoliberal turn often focusses on the role of various think tanks and institutes that were set up to promote free-market ideas and what was called monetarism, a policy of restricting the money supply. But to see the return of free-market economics mainly as a victory for one set of ideas over another is to attribute too much power to ideas. The importance of free-market theory was to provide direction and justification to deeper trends. As Simon Clarke put it, 'The debate between monetarism and Keynesianism was not resolved in the seminar room, but on the political stage.'[164] He might have added, and on the streets and in the workplaces.

The new approach to economy and society was in fact adopted quite rapidly and willingly by the ruling class. It was a response to a set of crises that also opened up new possibilities. By the early 1970s, the dominant semi-Keynesian model of the mixed economy was broken. The oil price shock of 1973 triggered a combination of stagnation and high inflation. Monetarism was presented as a way out of the crisis by countering inflation and restoring efficiency. But, as it was also a way to reduce wages and public spending, it was hardly unwelcome to the elites. As Alan Budd, an economic advisor to Thatcher's government, admitted some years later:

There may have been people making the actual policy

71

decisions... who never believed for a moment that this was the correct way to bring down inflation. They did however see that (monetarism) would be a very, very, good way to raise unemployment, and raising unemployment was an extremely desirable way of reducing the strength of the working classes.[165]

Labour's role in the 1970s had ended up having some uses for the ruling class. A right-wing government wouldn't have been able to ride out the anger generated by the cuts for so long. What is more, the disillusion with statism that resulted helped to create the conditions in which Thatcher could win an election. Winning office in 1979 was, however, just the beginning. Two years into her first term, after the first round of relatively mild cuts, polls showed Thatcher was running the most unpopular government since records began, with an approval rating of just 16 per cent.[166] She was rescued partly by the right-wing split from Labour that led to the SDP. The split confused and demoralised Labour supporters and divided the anti-Tory vote. Enthusiasm in some circles for the war to keep the Falkland Islands under British control also helped her win the 1983 election. The decimation of jobs caused by cuts helped demoralise trade unionists and Labour's wider political base. Cheap council house and utility sell-offs helped to buy her some support and gave some credibility to her free-market ideas.

Two other things, though, were absolutely essential to Thatcher's survival. The first was her successful assault on the trade unions. Attacks on steel workers, miners, printers and dockers in the first half of the 1980s were part of a careful plan developed before Thatcher came to office. In 1977, the Tory Economic Reconstruction Group chaired by Nicholas Ridley produced a strategy for widespread de-nationalisation. Its secret plan was leaked to the press and contained a 'confidential annex' which outlined preparations to take on the unions.

These included legal changes to stop strikers claiming benefits, stockpiling to undermine strikes, the organisation of non-union lorry drivers 'who are prepared to cross picket lines', and the creation of 'a large mobile squad of police who are equipped and prepared to uphold the law'. The document is couched in the terms of class war. The plan was to destroy resistance to privatisation by picking off weaker unions before confronting the main centres of working-class power.[167]

The Ridley plan was implemented with great success. The steel workers were taken on and beaten in 1979, then in 1983 a first assault against the printers' union followed at a new plant in Warrington. The police used the dispute to try out the techniques and technology of their new riot squads. They managed to disperse a mass picket of about 4,000. The next day, the *Financial Times* expressed satisfaction, 'the police tactics at Warrington… show clearly that they have learnt the lesson of mass picketing over the last ten years'.[168]

The year-long confrontation with the miners was the decisive battle. The dispute involved 150,000 workers in one of the longest strikes in history. It dominated politics and divided the country. Tens of thousands of working-class activists threw themselves into a magnificent campaign to support the strikers. But by the time the miners' dispute started in 1984, large amounts of coal had been stockpiled and a huge paramilitary police deployment prepared. As Seumas Milne, the author of a history of the strike, wrote on its tenth anniversary, the state responded with full-spectrum mobilisation:

It wasn't just the militarised police occupation of the coalfields; the 11,000 arrests, deaths, police assaults, mass jailings and sackings; the roadblocks, fitups and false prosecutions… under the prime minister's guidance, MI5, police, Special Branch, GCHQ and the NSA were mobilised not only to spy on the NUM on an industrial scale, but to employ agents provocateurs at the highest level of the union, dirty tricks, slush funds, false allegations, forgeries, phoney cash deposits and multiple secretly sponsored legal actions to break the defence of the mining communities.[169]

Despite this onslaught, defeat was far from inevitable. Papers in the national archives show that on at least two occasions, when action spread to other unions, Margaret Thatcher and close colleagues feared that she was on the brink of being brought down. She was only saved by the fact that supportive strikes were called off.[170]

The second thing that allowed Thatcher to sustain her project was the attitude of the Labour Party leadership. Neil Kinnock had taken over as leader in 1983. Despite the involvement of thousands of Labour Party members in the solidarity effort for the miners, he refused to back the strike. More generally, he and his colleagues responded to Thatcher's aggression by bending to it. Labour-supporting intellectuals were arguing that the Labour Party had to relate to what they saw as new realities.[171] Kinnock and his advisors agreed that the party needed to tack right in order to stay in the game. They embraced share ownership, talked up entrepreneurship and downplayed class: 'them and us are gone now' Kinnock said, 'we are all in this together'.[172] On issue after issue Labour fell into line. In a 1986 joint publication with the TUC, the Labour Party embraced some of Thatcher's anti-union laws. Even the *Financial Times* was surprised:

> Never before has the Labour Party, created by the unions, attempted to bring in controls of trade union activities on the scale proposed in the document. Never before has Labour tried to make that control statutory, backing it up, albeit now in a modified form – with the involvement of the courts, traditionally seen within the Labour movement as its enemy.[173]

The effect was the opposite of that intended. By ditching alternatives to Thatcher's free market, Labour demoralised working-class people and undermined hope in change. The resulting political disengagement allowed the Tories to stumble on, even after Thatcher had gone. Neil Kinnock managed to lose a second election in 1993 despite accumulated hatred for Thatcher and the tremendous success of the anti-Poll Tax movement, which had killed the tax and helped bring Thatcher down.

Labour also played a vital role in neoliberalism's second phase, which was partly a response to the dysfunction of the first. Tony Blair won the 1997 election on a landslide because of popular contempt for the Tories and their policies. Ironically, though, the election marked the point at which the Labour Party fully embraced the free market and liberalism. To underline the point, Blair had wanted to bring some Liberal MPs into his cabinet. Only the scale of his victory stopped him. Helped by a mini-boom, his government stabilised the regime, consolidating and expanding the financial sector's influence while at the same time rolling out some mildly progressive social policies. Whereas under Thatcher market reforms went awkwardly hand in hand with flag waving and 'family values', Blair married globalisation to a modernising social agenda that included gay rights, the rhetoric of women's liberation and a tepid multiculturalism. There was some increase in welfare spending but workers were largely ignored. The social role of some of the middle classes changed. Whereas for years some of the professional classes had helped to smooth relations between capital and the working class, now many were drawn towards the business of money making for its own sake, as 'a liberal mediation between capital and labour was no longer desirable or necessary'.[174] Neoliberalism had a short breakout moment. For a period, it was fashionable to believe that the welfare state would actually be enhanced by further openings towards the market and that a Labour government could be progressive while also being 'intensely comfortable with getting filthy rich as long as they pay their taxes'.[175]

Elite euphoria was short lived. The Iraq War exposed the extent to which Blair was locked into a special relationship with a more and more aggressive US elite, fascinated with a vision of a 'civilising' post-colonial global role, and contemptuous of popular opinion and parliament in pursuing these. Britain had been an unusually internationalised economy for some time, but now London was becoming the epicentre of overloaded networks of international financial speculation creating a casino economy of tax avoidance and corruption.

Not only had huge chunks of welfare and services been handed over to private companies, but households everywhere were becoming dependent on private debt to access essential services including housing, health, education and transport. The 2008 banking crisis ushered in the third phase of neoliberalism in Britain and brought to public attention just how complicit the state was in the economic regime. The state rescued the very banks that had precipitated the crisis. Brown's 'post boom and bust' Labour government pumped state funds into the banks and wrote off their bad assets, guaranteed deposits and engineered a zero-interest rate policy to try and restore liquidity. This led to a quadrupling of public debt from 36 per cent of GDP in 2006-07 to almost 150 per cent in 2010-11, an increase which became the central justification for austerity.[176]

A state transformed

The state had, in fact, been promoting big finance for years. This was never just about scrapping competition and credit controls, or deregulating markets. State institutions have helped pressure international debtors and set up free trade agreements, imposed rules on public spending and insisted on competitive tendering and balanced budgets.[177] Freed from any democratic control, the 'independent' Bank of England provided all sorts of services to the private banking sector, including circulating information about solvency and accounts. It offered private banks unlimited equity, sustaining continuous rises in asset values and allowing consumer debt to become the driver of economic growth.[178] The state that emerged was marked not just by a tight relationship with the banks but by a huge increase in the direct involvement of big business. The outsourcing of services to the private sector is only one part of this, but its scale and reach is startling. The National Audit Office estimated that by 2018, 50 per cent of total government spending on goods and services (£93.5 billion) went on third party providers.[179]

> Private sector involvement is heaviest in IT, construction, waste disposal, transport, building, facilities management, social care, military equipment and energy supply. Companies reach deep into national defence, training RAF pilots and servicing nuclear weapons. Bristow, a defence contractor based in Houston, Texas, has taken charge of UK search and rescue operations. Preparations for Trooping the Colour are in the hands of Vinci, the French construction company. Capita collects the London congestion charge and sends out television licence detector vans. Contractors, often subsidiaries of multinationals, run accommodation for asylum seekers, applications for UK visas, prisons and custody suites in police stations, refuse and waste disposal, school building (and till recently school inspection in England) as well as NHS community, mental and sexual health services.[180]

Locally and nationally, outsourcing has decimated workforces committed to delivering services. Their disappearance has been a disaster for the millions who rely on public services. Outsourcing guarantees that the implementation of services is determined by the profit motive rather than by the needs of users. In the process, it has also removed potential levers for change. But the problems go much deeper. The state has integrated business directly into its core functions. 'Quangos', unelected and often industry-funded bodies, have more and more control of state operations. As George Monbiot has documented, these bodies are often run by people with private interests who are 'blatantly biased'. They are also completely outside democratic control.[181] One study explains: 'The quango state removes layers and areas of policy-making and action from parliamentary – and public – gaze. The absence of a constitutional framework and the informal and secretive nature of its policy process blocks scrutiny and parliamentary and public debate about policy goals and outcomes.'[182]

Thatcher consciously marketised remaining parts of the civil service in a series of measures culminating in the 'next steps initiative'. These involved breaking the service up into over 100 autonomous agencies, or 'production units', each one directed by a head paid by performance and free to sub-contract to the private sector. The chief executives of these agencies have enormous power, undermining democracy and leading to what Labour MP Gerald Kaufman called 'the creeping abnegation of ministerial responsibility'.[183] The process was accelerated under Blair's government, which imported business expertise into government at levels unprecedented in peacetime.[184]

It is now normal to involve businesses directly and formally in government policy-making. In 2010, the Conservative Health Minister abolished the Food Standards Agency and invited Pepsico, Starbucks, McDonalds, Unilever, the Wine and Spirits Trade Association and other companies to help set public health policy. In 2011, a so-called 'buddy' scheme was introduced for 38 companies in trade and industry, giving them a 'direct line to ministers and officials'.[185] By the end of 2012, the original 38 companies – more than two-thirds of which are based outside the UK – had held a total of 700 face-to-face meetings with ministers.[186] The privatisation of policy-making reached its logical conclusion in March 2012, when the Tory Cabinet Secretary, at the top of the state's policy-making structure, suggested opening up policy-making itself to an external bidding process.[187]

The close integration with business is reflected in the type of people who now run the civil service. Whereas in the past, government ministries prided themselves on internal career paths and their leaders' commitment to service, by 2012, of the 200 most senior civil servants, 41 per cent had been recruited from outside the service, almost all from the private sector. The flow goes in both directions. A steady stream of senior bureaucrats and ministers now go on to highly-paid corporate jobs in the sector covered by their former departments.[188]

All this has also had a predictable blowback on parliament. For one thing, our political class has narrowed. *How Posh is Parliament?*, a Channel 4 News review of politicians' origins, found that over half had come from backgrounds in politics, law, business or finance. More MPs come from finance alone than from social work, the military, engineering and farming put together.[189] Politics is now more and more seen as a career rather than any kind of service. The results are disastrous. Growing careerism in Blair's Labour Party, for example, was directly linked to a willingness to cut welfare.[190]

In his memoirs, Brown aide Damian McBride gave an alarming insight into the resulting state of parliamentary life in the years after Blair:

It's the cut throat competition to be selected, elected and promoted, and the macho bear pit of parliamentary debate; it's the booze fuelled largesse and late nights of Westminster, and the ever growing distance from the people that put you there; it's the worship of money, praise and favour and the desperate kowtowing to those – including the media – who dispense them; it's the short-term motives behind most decision making and the partisan impulse to disagree for disagreement's sake... it encourages vanity, duplicity, greed, hypocrisy and cruelty. It rewards those whose instincts are reactionary and ruthless.[191]

Outsourcing sovereignty

If the state has handed significant control to business at home, it has also given up powers to international bodies. In the last 2 decades in particular, trans-state organisations have become more and more central to the functioning of the international system. Organisations like the G20, the IMF and the WTO have played a vital role in imposing neoliberal rules in different parts of the world. The USA and other Western powers have used them to ensure the safety of loans by insisting on tough repayment plans and linking them with foreign investment opportunities. But trans-state organisations are also often joined voluntarily by states as a way of outsourcing the job of imposing neoliberal norms. This has been a useful means for Western governments to discipline their own populations, while deflecting anger. The EU is one of these institutions. In general, free-trade areas tend to weaken corporations' concern with any social contract with its base population. In the words of Herman Daly in 1993:

> The broader the free-trade area, the less answerable a large and footloose corporation will be to any local or even national community. Spatial separation of the places that suffer the costs and enjoy the benefits becomes more feasible. The corporation will be able to buy labor in the low-wage markets and sell its products in the remaining high-wage high-income markets. The larger the market, the longer a corporation will be able to avoid the logic of Henry Ford, who realised that he had to pay his workers enough for them to buy his cars.[192]

Free-trade zones also tend to build in regulations that outlaw state intervention of various kinds. EU law and policy radically limits nation states' economic policy options. They insulate the member states from democratic pressures by making economic policy appear to be apolitically imposed by market rules.[193] By transferring some of their powers to supranational bodies, national governments are actually giving themselves some political space to withstand pressure from below. The EU's guiding principles clearly spell out that member states are obliged to conduct economic policy, 'in accordance with the principle of an open market economy with free competition'.[194] In the words of Kevin Featherstone, 'binding EU commitments enable governments to implement unpopular reforms at home whilst engaging in "blameshift" towards the EU, *even if they themselves had desired such policies'*.[195]

The EU has been controversial in Britain since it was founded. The British ruling class has historically been divided on its approach to the European Union, one wing backing a trade policy focussed on the former imperial territories of the so-called Commonwealth and a close relationship with the USA, the other pushing for deeper integration in Europe. In conditions of growing polarisation, the question of continued membership has detonated a full-blown political crisis. Britain's international decline and the growing importance of finance have meant that the overwhelming majority of British banking and big business now support EU membership. This has created turmoil by breaking apart the globalisation and Little England attitudes at Thatcherism's heart. The result has been that big business found itself in direct conflict with the membership of its main political party on a crucial question of economic policy. As if this was not bad enough, David Cameron's attempt to 'modernise' Toryism was frustrated by a popular revolt. The Brexit referendum ended up expressing a growing sense of alienation from Westminster politics, of the impact of globalisation and of sovereignty slipping away. Only by understanding the Brexit crisis as an intersection between elite division and popular discontent can we begin to chart a way forward.

The dangers of decline

Foreign policy has affected the British state in other ways. Few will need to be reminded of Tony Blair's enthusiastic military interventions and the disasters in Afghanistan and Iraq. But Blair's behaviour was far from an aberration. David Cameron spoke for the whole of the British establishment when, soon after his 2010 election, he outlined Britain's ambition to 'remain a major player in the world' by being 'one of only a handful of countries with the military, technological and logistical means to deploy serious military force around the world'.[196] Since then, Britain has played an important role in the assault on Libya and the war in Syria and backed and armed Saudi Arabia in its brutal assault in Yemen. It has kept as close as possible to Trump's confrontational foreign policy in the Pacific and in Eastern Europe and insisted that Britain will continue to be a 'global nation'.[197]

In the context of Britain's long-term decline, an air of fantasy surrounds these kinds of statements. But elite support for continued power projection is based on more than imperial nostalgia. Britain has the highest level of outward foreign direct investment in Europe and the second highest of all the G7 countries.[198] Its key earners, the finance and energy sectors, depend especially on the state's ability to project power and influence globally. Given the reality of Britain's declining world position, this means staying close to the USA. Arguing for a hike in military spending, the 2018 defence select committee put the case bluntly: 'diminished capacity reduces the UK's usefulness to the USA and our influence within NATO. The government must not allow this to happen.' The committee was backed up by former chief of staff Lord Nick Houghton, who argued that particularly in the light of the Brexit vote, the country needed to be very clear about its real priorities: 'More funding for health can win you tactical advantage in domestic elections but they don't enhance Britain's influence, power and respect in the world if that is the sort of country we want to be.'[199]

This is an unusually blunt statement of the dominant view of British capital's representatives. But the elites' addiction to war and their inability to accept the end of empire have helped generate popular discontent. The unprecedented movement against the Iraq War, involving Britain's biggest ever demonstration and the largest international protest in history, still reverberates. Every subsequent military intervention has been contested; most have been opposed by the vast majority of the population. What is more, for a state literally born out of coercion and empire, imperial decline is particularly dangerous and even risks an unravelling. Scottish independence has come closer than ever in the aftermath of the Iraq fiasco, with a removal of Trident missiles from Scottish soil a major demand. The fact that Jeremy Corbyn was a key figure in the Stop the War Coalition was a factor in his shock election as Labour's leader. Labour now has its first anti-war leader since the 1930s. There is a debate in Labour about foreign wars, the special relationship with the USA and even support for the Palestinian cause, opening up the possibility of a sharp change of foreign policy.

Another outcome of the wars is the growing importance of the military and security services in public and political life. In the run up to and during the Iraq War, Tony Blair met Richard Dearlove, the head of MI6, and Chair of the Joint Intelligence Committee, John Scarlett, privately before every cabinet meeting. As Peter Hennessy explains, 'It was quickly appreciated in post-9/11 Whitehall that thanks to Scarlett's and Dearlove's access to the Prime Minister, British intelligence had secured a more central place at the top decision-making tables to a degree unseen since the most perilous moments of the Cold War.'[200] Alastair Campbell liked to call John Scarlett his 'mate', perhaps not surprisingly given the fact that Scarlett stood by both Blair and Campbell over the misuse of deliberately distorted intelligence. Despite the disasters facilitated by this propaganda fix, Tony

Blair went on to make John Scarlett head of MI6. The continuing pursuit of the military option, and the spread of terrorism that has been one of its many pernicious results, has further raised the profile of military and security experts. Members of the secret services and 'security correspondents' are regulars on TV news bulletins.[201] Generals and ex-generals are routinely canvassed for their views on foreign policy and sometimes wider issues in the media. The generals and the security services are warming to their role. Just one week after Jeremy Corbyn's election as Labour leader, a serving general of the army was quoted in the *Observer*, warning of a direct and public challenge if a future Prime Minister Corbyn jeopardised the country's security: 'The army wouldn't stand for it... people would use whatever means possible, fair or foul to prevent that.'[202]

Growing international tensions have given the military the opportunity to move directly into the business of forming opinion. In March 2019, documents were leaked to the *Guardian* showing that the British military is recruiting philosophers, psychologists and theologians to develop new methods of psychological warfare and behaviour manipulation. Cambridge University was one of the bodies shortlisted by officials to partner the Ministry of Defence in spending around £70 million for a project known as the Human and Social Sciences Research Capability. The aim is to research how the arts, humanities and social sciences can help with the development of military and security strategies, including 'psychological operations'.[203] Almost inevitably, such projects will have a domestic as well as a foreign affairs remit. The Scottish company Integrity Initiative, which is partly funded by the Foreign and Commonwealth Office, is supposed to specialise in 'countering Russian online propaganda', but at the end of 2018 it was caught labelling Jeremy Corbyn as a 'useful idiot' for Moscow on its Twitter feed.[204]

Foreign wars and growing international tensions have made 'security' a buzzword in British politics, with toxic effects.

The demonisation of Muslims as an enemy within, mainly to justify wars, has helped create a situation in which the Muslim population feels under siege and Islamophobia has become the most virulent form of racism in British society. Some of the techniques of occupation used in Iraq and Afghanistan have been turned against domestic populations, just as 'lessons learnt' in Ireland were used on the streets of British cities in the 1980s against black communities. The increased bitterness against the West and the spread of terrorism which are outcomes of the wars have re-enforced demonisation and harassment of Muslims at home.

In a state more and more outsourced to commercial interests and less and less prepared to provide basic welfare, surveillance and monitoring have partially replaced state provision. Surveillance has, in fact, become central to the state's relationship with citizens, and the security services are at the heart of it. While commercially-based information gathering is built into an increasingly data-based economy, Edward Snowden's Wikileaks revelations exposed the extraordinary extent to which the British security services are working with online corporations to monitor our lives. Between 2008 and 2010, the leaks showed that with the help of the US National Security Agency, Britain's surveillance agency GCHQ intercepted and stored webcam images – including sexually explicit material – of millions of internet users who were not suspected of any wrongdoing. In one 6-month period in 2008 alone, the agency collected webcam imagery from more than 1.8 million Yahoo user accounts.[205]

Spending on public order more than tripled between 1979 and 2010.[206] It has fallen back a little since then, though this slack has probably been more than made up for by the burgeoning private security business. Once again, London has been the testing ground for new strategies of policing the poor. After the 2011 riots, the Metropolitan Police imported the 'total policing' model pioneered by William Bratton, a former

New York Police Commissioner, following the policy of zero tolerance and 'escalating force'.[207] This strategy and others adopted elsewhere are based on 'pre-emptive policing', in which police target groups according to whether they are 'likely' to commit a crime or engage in disorder. These policies involve the use of covert policing methods, running agents, using 'secret evidence' and other dubious and arguably illegal methods. As one investigation into current policing methods suggests, we are faced with a 'hybrid criminal justice system' based on a mix of policing methods that 'blur the lines between the police and the military, civil law and martial law' in line with 'a hybrid crime/ war framework'.[208]

States of mind

All this has been accompanied by an extraordinary self-certainty in ruling circles. Encouraged by the insulation from the majority of the population provided by soaring inequality, neoliberal ideas have taken hold with the force of religion. Any challenge to the dogma of globalisation is tellingly dismissed as 'populism'. The state broadcaster, the BBC, has become evangelical in its defence of EU membership and systematically contemptuous of Corbyn and his supporters. Researchers have found that during 2015, BBC evening news bulletins gave nearly twice as much unchallenged airtime to voices critical of Corbyn than to those that supported him and that the Labour leadership and its supporters were persistently referred to in ways that suggested hostility, intransigence and extreme positions.[209] The BBC appears to have become an organising centre for the project of destabilising the Corbyn leadership. A leading QC claims he has evidence that BBC producers have been routinely trying to undermine Corbyn by portraying him as too old and stupid to deal with the complexities of the job.[210]

For some commentators, the state's identification with the neoliberal order suggests that neoliberalism is an all-encompassing regime in which market rationality has come to dominate the population completely.[211] The logic of this kind of analysis is that neoliberalism is so embedded in society that it can't be dislodged. In their widely acclaimed recent study of neoliberalism, for example, Dardot and Laval argue that its 'tour de force' has been the successful production of 'the neo-liberal subject', the citizen who has completely internalised market rationality. They suggest that Thatcher has succeeded in her aim of 'changing the heart and soul' of the population.[212]

There is no question that a state so tied up with business interests, practices and attitudes presents more obstacles than ever to progressive change. But it is important to distinguish between the stubborn adherence to neoliberal principle amongst the elites and the state of mind of the wider population.[213] The corporatised state has, in fact, generated widespread discontent. Partly this is because it has become virtually incapable of carrying out what Marx identified as one of its basic roles of keeping society functioning. But the series of mass movements and rebellions, from the Iraq War protests, anti-austerity marches, the near-miss Scottish independence vote, the vote to leave the EU in 2016 and the rise of Jeremy Corbyn, have all expressed a deeper anxiety still. It is clear that millions of ordinary people feel they have lost whatever limited control they had over society and that the state is completely oblivious and even hostile to their interests and concerns. The Corbyn phenomenon has channelled discontent through the parliamentary system but in a peculiarly insurgent way that reflects Corbyn's long record of extra-parliamentary campaigning. It is seen as an existential threat by the Labour Party Right and, as reported by the *Financial Times*, big business is more afraid of a Corbyn government than it is of Brexit. As FT columnist Merryn Somerset Webb said of the policy of quantitative easing (QE) which rescued the banks: 'You hear the result of QE in the UK every time the shadow chancellor John McDonnell opens his mouth demanding a socialist reset – and he appears to have the support of about 40% of the population.'[214]

The Brexit fiasco has been so spectacular and damaging because Brexit is an expression of a general crisis of the British state. As we have seen, the referendum detonated growing tensions in the Tory Party. What made matters much worse was that it also channelled the deep popular discontent with the Westminster elites and the whole experience of neoliberalism and foreign wars. The result was an extraordinary situation in which a Tory government had to try to implement a policy that was directly opposed to the strategy of big finance and the dominant corporations. The usual escape route in times of difficulty, bringing in a Labour government, was closed off by the fact of Corbyn's leadership, another reaction against the neoliberal establishment.

The ruling class is deeply divided and seems unable to take society forward. The dominant economic project remains the financialised globalisation that has created the problems in the first place. In its decline, the ruling class appears to have forgotten many of the lessons that it learnt since it began to accommodate democracy in the second half of the nineteenth century. It appears less and less interested in making concessions, responding to popular concerns or maintaining the appearance of neutrality. The Blairites' enthusiastic embrace of the free market in the 1990s weakened Labour's traditional ability to channel discontent relatively safely through the institutions. It has led to the development of a new Left in a series of mass movements against war and austerity that has powered Corbyn's insurgent leadership of Labour. In the process, it has created the biggest chance for fundamental change in generations.

Chapter Six

Making the Break

Capital is the extra-parliamentary force par excellence.
Istvan Meszaros[215]

For more than 200 years, the British state has actively and consciously defended the interests of the owners of capital. Illusions of gradualism and state neutrality have been encouraged by the ruling elites at the same time as they have repressed resistance, limited the power of parliament and structured democracy in ways that make change harder. There have, at times, been serious tensions between the various elements in the ruling bloc and these have encouraged resistance from below, which has been the main motor of change. But despite moments of extreme crisis, during the nineteenth and most of the twentieth century, there has been a growing convergence of elite interests, a consolidation of the ruling bloc and a gradual professionalisation of the state. The elites were able to overcome internal division and have known when to make concessions, when to use force and how best to combine the two, all the time claiming change to be a product of their own enlightened policy.

This survival act was, however, only possible because at the moment when the British establishment was finally forced to concede the vote, a political vehicle had emerged that claimed to represent working people but was blind to the influence and power of the state. From the moment it was founded, the Labour Party accepted the separation between politics and economics and unquestioningly respected the state institutions that had done so much to keep working people down. After the Second World War, as a result of years of struggle and popular discontent, Labour was able to secure a new settlement in which the state was finally forced to make significant concessions to working people. The state was not, however, fundamentally democratised. The separation between politics and economics was maintained and the basic structure of capitalist accumulation was undisturbed. The unelected parts of the state continued to be deployed regularly against popular resistance. On the few occasions when Labour governments looked like they might overstep lines, the state has moved against them too. At other moments, mass movements have opened up new avenues for possible change. But these movements have not been able to develop an approach capable of dealing with hostile state institutions. The result has been that Labour's tacit acceptance of the political limits set by the state has contained popular aspirations for fundamental change.

These patterns that have served the British capitalist class so well for so long are breaking down under the stress accumulated in the years of neoliberalism. The current regime of globalisation is no more the product of blind market forces than was the liberal order of the nineteenth century. Corporate entities didn't steal power in the late 1970s in a takeover. As Susan Strange puts it, 'they had it handed to them on a plate'.[216] Enormous economic, political and social effort has been expended on imposing free-market principles, supporting big business and finance, and limiting democratic control over the markets. International bodies including the EU have been handed powers to enforce free-market rules. Where services have not been given over wholesale to the corporations, market logic has been imposed across the civil service and enforced by centralised monitoring. All this has eroded what little democratic control existed and concentrated power at the top of unelected state institutions. It will make the task of changing society through the institutions harder than ever. But these very same developments have helped to create a deep crisis in the state. They have split the Conservative Party, eroded faith in capitalism's core institutions and led to a deep and wide questioning of the nature of our political regime.

State of denial

Despite these developments, the Left still often sidesteps the questions posed by the power of the state. In Paul Mason's account of how we reach 'post capitalism', for example, the state is barely discussed. Instead, following in a long tradition, he argues that capitalism can be transcended by new technological developments.[217] Elsewhere, Mason argues, oddly, that the years of neoliberalism have tamed the state:

> If there is one upside to 30 years of free-market economics in Britain, it is the strengthening of the rule of law. Britain has not only the Human Rights Act and a Supreme Court, but a state which operates consciously within legal checks and balances. From the audio recorders in police interview rooms to the legal hotline for drone pilots at RAF Waddington, there is pervasive legal supervision. The shenanigans of the 1970s, when MI5 'bugged and burgled' the Wilson government; or in the 1980s, when the Association of Chief Police Officers co-ordinated the systematic denial of freedom of movement to striking miners, would be much harder to get away with today.[218]

Another response on the Left is simply to reassert the idea of state intervention as a virtue in the teeth of free-market fundamentalism. In one of the most interesting recent books about the state, Mitchell and Fazi argue that the crisis of Keynesianism was a result of intervention not going far enough and a failure to confront the logic of globalisation. Their *Reclaiming the State* exposes the ideological nature of neoliberal economic assumptions and its conclusions are optimistic and radical. Mitchell and Fazi argue for a comprehensive policy of nationalisation including public, democratic ownership of the banks, collective goods, popular rule and egalitarian welfarism.[219]

This is a refreshing change after the years of pessimism induced by neoliberal myths of market mastery. But Mitchell and Fazi barely discuss the problems posed by the interests embedded in the state. Radical reforming governments can make real improvements in working people's lives, give confidence to activists, popularise socialist ideas and deepen elite crisis. But to avoid disaster, it is crucial to be clear about the resistance these projects will face and to develop strategies to deal with it. This is particularly important at a time when the establishment is responding to challenges by digging in rather than changing course. Its inflexibility is structural. It is a product of relative economic decline and low levels of profits which make redistribution unattractive. It is also a result of the central importance of global financial circuits to the British economy and the highly internationalised nature of its core businesses. The resulting intransigence is going to mean that, should a radical government be elected, it would find itself on a collision course not just with big business and the banks but with the core institutions of the British state. The outcome is likely to be an attempt at a slow coup involving action on many fronts: attacks on the pound, investment flight, civil service sabotage, further media witch-hunts and smears in collaboration with the Right in Labour, all backed up with threats and heavy lobbying from the police and the military.

There is now in some quarters signs of a readiness to consider these challenges. There has recently been some criticism of the reluctance of Labour leaders to discuss capital controls and other radical economic measures publicly.[220] A suggestion which has gained some traction is that the Left will have to work 'in and against the state', and that real change will require popular mobilisations and activism, including by workers employed by the state.[221] The supporters of this strategy draw on a number of theoretical resources. They often cite particular interpretations of Gramsci's *Prison Notebooks*, and the theoretical work of Greek socialist Nicos Poulantzas.[222] Both of them shared the view that the state in 'advanced' capitalist societies was more developed and resilient than that of the nineteenth century, in particular the Russian state that was overthrown by the Bolsheviks in 1917. For Gramsci, the priority was the development of a bloc or alliance of progressive forces, led by the most advanced sections of the working class, organised in the 'Modern Prince', his euphemism for revolutionary organisation. Such struggles could loosen the hold of ruling-class ideas and control over the lives of the population. These were ideas that drew on the theory and practice of the united front promoted particularly by the Russian revolutionaries Lenin and Trotsky as capitalism began to re-stabilise in Europe in the years after the Russian Revolution.

Writing in the 1970s, Poulantzas was more critical of the Marxist tradition. He argued that the state shouldn't be seen simply as an active agent of social forces. In *State, Power, Socialism* he developed the notion of the state as a product of power struggles in society, 'the condensation of a relationship of forces' rather than as a set of institutions to defend a particular class regime. In his view, the state was open to influence by the working class: 'The state is a strategic field ploughed from one end to the other by the working class and popular resistance.'[223] For Poulantzas, any process of transformation would take place largely within the state structures through 'the spreading, development, co-ordination and direction of those diffuse centres of resistance which the masses always possess within the state networks'.[224]

The state *has* grown in complexity as capitalism has developed. Both its economic and its social role expanded dramatically in the twentieth century, especially in the decades after the Second World War. By the 1970s, a wide range of state institutions affected many aspects of the lives of the whole population, although its social role has receded since. These changes were partly forced on the ruling class by popular pressure. But in his early exploration of the Western capitalist state, Antonio Gramsci never suggested that the state had ceased to defend the interests of the ruling elite. His point was that, under pressure, capitalists had discovered *more* stable and effective ways of ruling, involving a range of institutions that promoted ruling-class ideas and attitudes and produced the appearance of consent while protecting class power.

Central to this was his elaboration of Marx's insight into the impact of the separation of politics and economics. Parliamentary democracy treats people as individual citizens with equal rights when they vote every few years. In between times, in the workaday world which Gramsci called 'civil society', people's existence is shaped by a highly exploitative and hierarchical economic system over which parliament has little control. This division between the political world and civil society, combined with the impact of welfare, education and media, is central to generating a level of consent in capitalist society. Developing the theme, Marxist philosopher Istvan Meszaros has pointed out how in Britain this process discounted the most effective weapon that working people have. The Labour Party, by taking on the role of 'political arm' of the movement, confines the unions to strictly economic labour disputes. It thus plays into capital's vital interest, 'to ban "politically motivated industrial action" as categorically inadmissible "in a democratic society".'[225]

Poulantzas' claim that the state is 'ploughed from one end to another' by workers' struggles is an exaggeration which underestimates the extent to which the state serves the interests of the ruling elites. Downplaying conscious ruling-class agency in state organisation risks disorientating people. For all its complexity, the history of the British state bears out the argument that Marx made and Lenin developed, and which Miliband later elaborated, that the capitalist state's abiding preoccupation and key organising principle is imposing and sustaining class rule. How else can we explain the way the state was used to help impose the factory system, repress protest and tame democracy in the nineteenth century, the way it has continued to mobilise against all sorts of dissent since, its efforts to undermine Left governments and its role in imposing the neoliberal regime? How else to understand that even when it is engaged in projects not entirely dictated by immediate class interest, organising welfare, say, or administering the national education system, it does so in ways that actively promote the interests of the ruling elites? By underestimating class interest, purposefulness and co-ordination, a purely structural analysis tends to encourage the idea that state actors can be persuaded to change course or that state institutions can be neutralised or transformed over time, one by one. These are precisely the ideas that Labour politician R.H. Tawney warned against as he became radicalised through the experiences of Labour in office in the 1920s. Referring to the British state, he said, 'You can eat an onion leaf by leaf, but you cannot skin a live tiger paw by paw; vivisection is its trade and it does its skinning first.'[226]

This is not to suggest a special conspiracy, or a crudely instrumental view of the state. Conspiracy theories are often the result of people sensing elite collusion without understanding how deeply class shapes our institutions. Structure and agency come together in the state. It has been structured over time by the class that dominates society, in a society dominated by market relations. Co-ordination between different wings of the state and leaders of big business is built into that structure. As both Marx and Miliband recognised, it is not that capitalists directly run state institutions, although corporate input into state policy is rising rapidly. Rather, it is that they have ensured that the key institutions of the state are controlled by people who share their aims and interests, and that mechanisms of co-ordination are built in. This multi-level co-ordination is formally institutionalised, in the cabinet, in meetings of permanent Whitehall secretaries, at the COBRA emergency committee or the National Security Council meetings, for example. Other discussions between state leaders in different spheres and business representatives will take place out of sight and out of mind in the Carlton Club, at Chatham House and other think tanks, at business dinners or in media green rooms. As Miliband argued, such are the shared values, interests and instincts of those that control the various wings of the state that often they will act in unison without needing to communicate directly. The state does indeed employ hundreds of thousands of workers. As we have seen, there have been moments when even police and troops have rebelled. But these were times of wider insurgency. Since then, the key sectors of the state have been consciously reinforced. There would have to be generalised resistance across society to turn the strategic asset of the state's workforce to account. This, in turn, demands a wider movement which is clear about the state's role.

As neoliberal capitalism fails whole populations, there is a trend towards more authoritarian forms of rule across Europe and beyond. In periods in which a ruling group is capable of taking society forward, it is more likely to be able to 'spontaneously' generate a level of consensus in its own ranks and amongst opinion formers, and therefore some degree of consent in wider society. In conditions of retrenchment, decline and economic crisis, this is no longer the case and the ruling group's influence or hegemony is weakened. At these times the temptation will be to adopt more authoritarian forms of government. 'As soon as the dominant social group has exhausted its function,' Gramsci argued, 'the ideological bloc tends to crumble away; then "spontaneity" may be replaced by "constraint" in ever less disguised and indirect forms, culminating in outright police measures and *coups d'etat'*.[227]

The champions of neoliberal globalisation insist that the threat to democracy comes from outside their ranks, from what they call 'populists' and from nationalists of various kinds. It is true that the misery and alienation of neoliberal life has summoned up monsters as well as inspiring popular revolts and progressive movements. It is an urgent task to deal with the surge in far-right ideas and organisation. But it is important that in doing so we are not blinded to the fact that it is neoliberal governance that has created the conditions in which far-right ideas can flourish. Meanwhile, the political representatives of neoliberalism who have worked so hard to limit democracy over the years are quite capable of going much further down the road towards authoritarianism. Indeed, in some countries neoliberal governments are already embracing far-right movements. 'The extreme centre', as Tariq Ali has called it, is not above working with the far-right to maintain control. Dealing with it remains the central priority of any serious Left.

The vote and the street

A survey of moments of political crisis in bourgeois democracies shows that struggles for change always involve interaction between parliamentary politics and wider struggles and movements. In democracies, it is natural that the majority of the population will look at least partly to parliament for political change. Voting in elections is less daunting than the prospect of struggling to change the system. Parliamentary politics played a role in Italy in the Red Years of 1919-1920 and in the revolutionary period in Germany in the years after 1918. In France, it was central to the Popular Front crisis in the 1930s and to the resolution of the events of 1968. It was central again in the tragic history of Chile in the early 1970s and the more modest British crisis of the same decade. More recently, it has been a factor in the politics of the great popular explosions in Bolivia and Argentina at the start of this century and was, of course, crucial in the Syriza experience in Greece. Even in autocratic Russia in 1917, the politics of the semi-democratic national assembly or Duma was an important component in how the revolution played out. Despite the caricatures of Leninism, the Russian revolutionaries paid careful attention to electoral politics, and the parliamentary strategy was a vital if subordinate element in their strategy for achieving socialism.

It is important to be absolutely clear, however, that in all these cases, popular mobilisations played a central role. In some cases, where the struggle reached particularly high levels, the movement threw up new, participatory forms of democratic organisation rooted in workplaces and working-class communities. As well as the soviets that were at the heart of the Russian Revolution, there were factory councils in northern Italy in the Red Years, workers' councils in revolutionary Germany, *cordones* in Chile and popular assemblies in Argentina and Bolivia.[228] These organisations developed out of the immediate needs of the struggle, but they suggested the possibility of a more thoroughgoing form of democratic power than the parliamentary system ever allows. They challenged the separation between economics and politics, between everyday life and national political power. As Gramsci himself said, the Italian factory councils were 'the model of the proletarian state'.[229]

We are of course a long way from the kind of acute class polarisation of these high points of struggle. But it is worth noting that in all these cases, the moment when politics was reduced to what happened in parliament tended to be the moment at which forward progress was halted and the system began to stabilise. On the other hand, it was at the very highest points of mass struggle that previously unorganised staff working in offices, state institutions, banks, finance and so on began to take action and become radicalised. When millions of French workers took strike action and many occupied their factories in 1936 in support of a left government, the situation was clarified for millions of others in society. As one eye-witness put it:

The shop workers, the technicians who announce that they have no special demands to lodge but simply want to demonstrate their solidarity with their worker comrades, the women, the young girls so full of fight, the staffs of the insurance companies, the stock exchange and the banks, they all now understand that there is only one fight.[230]

Where they exist, anti-neoliberal electoral parties of the Left are bound to play an important part in future struggles for change. Getting such parties elected anywhere would be destabilising to a system wedded to neoliberal principles. Their election can help change political direction and raise expectations. That is why they will be met with concerted opposition from banks, corporations, the media and the whole array of state institutions.What is more, this struggle to neutralise or sabotage radical electoral projects starts before they take office. In Britain, establishment forces have been encouraging and enabling the right wing within Labour to overturn or dilute radical policy commitments ever since Jeremy Corbyn was elected leader in 2015. As a result, the Left has been forced to retreat from a whole range of important positions.

Simply standing on the sidelines and denouncing efforts to reform the system is pointless. It convinces next to no one and deprives radical initiatives of valuable active support. What is needed is the widest possible participation in the struggle for change based on a realistic assessment of how that change can actually happen. Precisely for this reason, just throwing ourselves into a left electoral project is also inadequate. Four principles are important to chart a way forward. The first is a firm commitment to a radical programme. Because neoliberalism is so embedded and because it has done so much damage, a reforming government that fails to act decisively and radically will end up making no headway and disappointing its support base. A completely new direction will be necessary to secure even modest change.

An incoming government would have to be prepared to introduce a tax regime that reverses inequality and releases the resources necessary to address the series of social problems that have built up during the neoliberal years. It must be prepared to nationalise key sectors of the economy to deliver functioning, free or affordable and environmentally-sustainable services. This will require publicly rejecting the idea that state-run industry or services are less efficient than private, and the notion of the corporations' right to make a profit wherever they see the main chance. It would mean setting up mechanisms to direct investment towards green and socially-useful industry and to divert resources away from arms manufactures and heavily polluting sectors. It would mean a sharp break from the interventionist foreign policy that has caused such mayhem internationally, tied us politically to Washington and wasted unimaginable wealth on devastating wars. It would mean breaking up the big banks and separating commercial and investment banking, to end the impossible situation in which 'too big to fail' banks are kept afloat by endless amounts of public money while operating as purely profit-seeking bodies. It would mean being prepared to use capital controls against speculative financial capital in general and the use of capital flight as a political weapon in particular. Only such a radical programme can begin to chart a course out of disaster and sustain confidence amongst the electorate that change is coming.

The second principle is that the state as it exists is not fit for this purpose. The current institutions of the state couldn't possibly carry through this programme. They are designed to do diametrically opposite things and to block any such developments. Given their record, we know they would be at the forefront of obstruction and sabotage. The health service, the public education system or what remains of the library service, say, could be reworked under a different leadership with popular participation. But it is hard to see how a genuinely radical government could approach the quango-ridden hierarchies at the very heart of the British civil service except with the aim of dismantling them. John McDonnell is right to say that a new unit will have to be set up to oversee the nationalisation of industries, as there is currently no mechanism for implementing any kind of economic planning that doesn't emanate from big business.[231] But it is naïve to think that the Treasury will accept orders to co-operate in nationalisation plans that are not endorsed by big business. It may reluctantly agree to consult with members of the public and trade unions in threatened 'listening exercises', it will perhaps grudgingly accept some wealth redistribution, but it won't countenance any democratic control over industry. A genuinely radical economic policy will require more than a few new units, it will need new structures altogether.

The third principle is that a radical programme will only stand a chance of success if it is backed by mass mobilisation outside parliament. Any attempt to transform the state will be resisted with even more energy than a radical economic agenda. We have seen the array of forces that were deployed against the plans of the Wilson government, plans which barely touched the mechanisms of state. They included corporate leaderships, bankers and the IMF, parts of the media, the civil service, the army and the security forces. We have seen, too, that the right wing of Labour is more loyal to the state and the status quo than it is to the democratically expressed wishes of the party itself. It will oppose any policies that throw into question management's right to manage or the dominant power of the corporations. Workers employed by the state can potentially help to implement change and push back against resistance, but given the huge resources at the state's command, the job can hardly be left to them alone. Dealing with the power of the state and the financial markets will require the deployment of immensely powerful social forces outside state institutions as a precondition for a struggle within.

The fourth principle that follows is there needs to be a strengthening of the extra-parliamentary Left. The necessary society-wide mobilisations of working people would involve many members of the Labour Party, but they will not be organised by the Labour Party itself, as this is not the party's purpose. Apart from anything else, Labour, despite being the biggest political party in Europe, organises a fraction of the working class. There are approximately 30 million working people in Britain, 7.5 million of whom are in unions. Extra-parliamentary mobilisation is not the Labour Party's priority. Its whole purpose is parliamentary change; it was, as we have seen, set up in response to setbacks to working-class self-activity in order to implement an alternative strategy, that of working within the institutions. This orientation shapes its structures, its traditions and its behaviour. All the pressure, even on the Left, is in the opposite direction; to self-present as statesmanlike, to behave in a parliamentary manner and to accept the strict division between politics and economics. It is a huge struggle for a left leadership to retain its commitment to a progressive political programme, even when backed by a broadly left membership. Organising mass resistance in the streets or the workplaces is simply not part of the plan. The election of a radical Labour government can electrify the popular mood and give confidence to activists, but it will not bring these people into the kind of participation in politics in the streets and in the workplaces that will be needed to force radical reforms through.

For this, another kind of activism and another kind of organisation is needed.

The only circumstances in which the Right can be pushed back permanently and new institutions can start to challenge existing structures of power are ones in which working people are mobilised, struggling for change and starting to take initiatives themselves. This demands not just organisation but strategy and therefore will require political organisation consciously focussed on organising change from below; on strengthening union activism, on extending the reach of the movements against austerity, racism and war into every community and on arguing for maximum popular participation and for the principle of self-emancipation.

Such an extra-parliamentary Left focussed on change from below is essential to defend and push forward a reforming government. It needs, of course, to work as closely as possible with left-wing Labour members. In the mid-1920s, the Communist Party initiated the Left-Wing Movement to form a bridge between activists inside and outside Labour, between revolutionaries and non-revolutionaries. Such organised co-operation between the Left inside and outside Labour is necessary again. But it will take a strong extra-parliamentary Left to initiate it.

A dynamic extra-parliamentary Left is also necessary to deepen the struggle for change in society at large. In one of his earliest discussions of the state, Marx remarked that it is related to wider society 'in the same way as heaven is to earth'.[232] He was moving towards the understanding of the state and political institutions as *products* of a divided, class-ridden society. The logic of this view is that a challenge to the state can only be successful if it is part of a struggle to transform the society that gives rise to it, by measures to extend popular control over the economy. Parliamentary politics can help to raise these questions, but because it has so little influence over the economy it cannot resolve them. Introducing democracy into the economic realm requires permanent, new ways of organising society that come from below which can break down the division between politics and economics. We mustn't be fooled again. Capital's domination and the power of the state that backs it up cannot be dismantled by parliamentary decree; they can only finally be overcome by the self-activity of working people.

Endnotes

1. Walter Bagehot (1894) *The English Constitution,* Kegan Paul, Trench, Trubner and Co., London, p.xxiii.
2. BBC TV comedy series *Yes, Prime Minister,* series 1 (1986-1988) episode 3, The Smoke Screen, 23 January 1986.
3. Karl Marx (1976) *Capital: Volume 1,* Penguin, London, p.874.
4. Anthony King (2015) *Who Governs Britain?* Penguin, London, p.280.
5. Martin Delgado, 'MI5 has secret dossiers on one in 160 adults', *The Mail on Sunday,* 9 July 2006.
6. Tony Benn (2005) *The Benn Diaries 1940-1990,* Random House, London, p.451.
7. Ellen Meiskins-Wood (1991) *The Pristine Culture of Capitalism: A Historical Essay on Old Regimes and Modern States,* Kindle Edition, Verso, London, Loc 527.
8. David Edgerton (2018) *The Rise and Fall of the British Nation,* Penguin, London, p.xxiv.
9. Anthony King (2015) *Who Governs Britain?* London, Penguin, p.188.
10. Christopher Hill (1991) *A Nation of Change and Novelty: Radical Politics, Religion and Literature in Seventeenth-Century England,* Bookmarks, London, p.23 and 24.
11. John Le Carre (2016) *The Pigeon Tunnel,* Penguin, London, p.19.
12. Ralph Miliband, 'How the Reasonable Men of Capitalism Orchestrated Horror in Chile 42 Years Ago Today', reposted on *Jacobin* 11 September 2015. Available at https://www.jacobinmag.com/2015/09/chile-coup-santiago-allende-social-democracy-september-11/
13. See for example, 'Trust, Politics and Institutions', *British Social Attitudes Survey 2013,* available at *http://www.bsa.natcen.ac.uk/latest-report/british-social-attitudes-30/key-*

findings/trust-politics-and-institutions.aspx

14. John McDonnell (ed.) (2018) *Economics for the Many*, London, Verso.

15. Paul Mason, 'Labour needs to wage war on EU neoliberalism to prevent a Brussels sabotage', *New Statesman*, 9 May 2018.

16. Karl Marx and Frederick Engels, 'Manifesto of the Communist Party' in *Marx and Engels: Basic Writings*, Lewis S. Feuer (ed) (1984) Fontana, London, p.51.

17. Karl Marx and Frederick Engels (1846) *The German Ideology*, Part 3, Political Liberalism. Available at https://www.marxists.org/archive/marx/works/1845/german-ideology/ch03d.htm

18. See K. Marx (1981) *Capital: Volume 3*, Penguin, London p.845.

19. Phillip Snowden (1913) *The Game of Party Politics*, ILP, London p.11. Available at https://babel.hathitrust.org/cgi/pt?id=wu.89119120632;view=1up;seq=17

20. Quoted in Simon Hannah (2018) *A Party with Socialists In It*, Pluto, London, p.6.

21. V.I. Lenin (1992) *State and Revolution*, Penguin, London, p.9.

22. Quoted in H. Mercer (1991) 'The Labour governments of 1945-1951 and private industry' in Nick Tiratsoo (ed) (1991) *The Attlee Years*. Pinter, London, p.84.

23. Ralph Miliband (1969) *The State in Capitalist Society*, Basic Books, New York, pp.49-50.

24. Nicos Poulantzas (1978) *Political Power and Social Classes*, Verso, London, p.48.

25. The debate between Miliband and Poulantzas took place in the *New Left Review*.
See Nicos Poulantzas (1969) 'The Problems of the Capitalist State' in *New Left Review* 1/58, November/December 1969 and Ralph Miliband (1970) 'The Capitalist State, Reply to N. Poulantzas' in *New Left Review* 1/59, January/February 1970. See also Ralph Miliband (1973) 'Poulantzas and

the Capitalist State' in *New Left Review*, 1/82, November/ December 1973.

26. To get a flavour of these discussions see Stuart Hall (1988) 'The Meaning of New Times' in Kuan-Hsing Chen and David Morley (eds) (1996) *Stuart Hall: Critical Dialogues in Cultural Studies*, Routledge, London, pp.223-237.

27. John Brewer (1989) *The Sinews of Power: War, Money and the English State 1688-1783*, e-Reader version, Unwin Hyman, London, Loc. 170.

28. William Mitchell and Thomas Fazi (2017) *Reclaiming the State: A Progressive Vision of Sovereignty for a Post-Neoliberal World*, Pluto, London, p.6.

29. As Ellen Meiksens Wood has pointed out this depoliticising retreat into identity involves rejecting the idea of totalising knowledge at a moment of triumph for 'the most totalizing system the world has ever known'. See her 1995 book, *Democracy Against Capitalism: Renewing Historical Materialism*, Cambridge University Press, Cambridge, p.2.

30. Antonio Gramsci (1971) *Selections from the Prison Notebooks*, Quintin Hoare and Geoffrey Nowell Smith (eds), Lawrence and Wishart, London, pp.323-324.

31. Edmund Burke (2003) *Reflections on the Revolution in France: And on the Proceedings in Certain Societies in London Relative to That Event*, London, Penguin, p.18.

32. David Nicholls (1988) 'A Subordinate Bourgeoisie? The Question of Hegemony in Modern British Capitalist Society', in Colin Barker and David Nicholls (eds), *The Development of British Capitalist Society*, Northern Marxists Historians Group, Manchester, p.51.

33. See E.P. Thompson's brilliant 1965 essay, 'The Peculiarities of the English', in *Socialist Register* 1965, p.328 Available here https://socialistregister.com/index.php/srv/issue/view/449 See also John Saville (1994) *The Consolidation of the Capitalist State 1800-1850*, London, Pluto, pp.48-51.

34. Bagehot, the leading nineteenth century expert on the British constitution, argued that maintaining an aristocratic or what he called 'dignified' part of the constitution was useful in keeping the masses in awe. It was a distraction from the real work being undertaken by the middle classes in the 'efficient' part. He went further and saw advantage in allowing the aristocrats a role in the 'efficient' part itself:
'As long as we keep up a double set of institutions...we should take care that the two match nicely, and hide where the one begins and where the other ends. This is in part effected by conceding some subordinate power to the august part of our polity, but it is equally aided by keeping an aristocratic element in the useful part of our polity.'
Quoted in E.P. Thompson's 1965 essay, 'The Peculiarities of the English', in *Socialist Register* 1965, p.328 Available here https://socialistregister.com/index.php/srv/issue/view/449

35. One of Adam Smith's great breakthroughs was to recognise that labour produced wealth. His views on the state were much more complex than many of his promoters let on. He believed for example that the state had an important role to play in offsetting market forces in some crucial areas. For more on this and how his ideas have been distorted, see John Saville (1994) *The Consolidation of The Capitalist State 1880-1850*, London, Pluto, p.36.

36. G. Slater (1913) 'Historical Outline of Land Ownership in England', in *The Land, The Report of the Land Enquiry Committee,* Hodder and Stoughton, London,

37. John Saville (1994) *The Consolidation of the Capitalist State 1800-1850*, London, Pluto, p.20.

38. See John Saville (1994), p.23.

39. See John Saville (1994), p.22.

40. The research has been carried out by the *Legacies of British Slave-ownership Centre* at University College London. The data is published on its website: https://www.ucl.ac.uk/lbs/

project/project

41. Quoted in Mark O'Brien (1995) *Perish the Privileged Orders: A Socialist History of the Chartist Movement.* London, Bookmarks, p.15.

42. Paul Foot (1984) *Red Shelley*, London, Bookmarks, p.36.

43. In March 1819, a few months before the protest, Henry Hobhouse, permanent undersecretary to the home secretary Lord Sidmouth, sent a private letter to a Bolton Magistrate telling him it was the 'opinion long since formed by his Lordship that your Country will not be tranquillised until Blood shall have been shed either by the Law or the sword. Lord Sidmouth will not fail to be prepared for either alternative.' See Katrina Navickas (2018) 'Opprobrious Epithets' in *London Review of Books*, Vol. 40, No. 24, 20 December 2018, pp.33-35.

44. Quoted in Finer, S.E. (1952) *The Life and Times of Sir Edwin Chadwick,* London, Methuen.

45. See John Saville (1994), p.63.

46. Quoted in John Saville (1994), p.44.

47. Quoted in Paul Foot (2005) *The Vote: How it Was Won and How it Was Undermined,* Penguin, London, p.68.

48. Quoted in Paul Foot (2005), pp.70-71.

49. Paul Foot (2005), p.80.

50. Adolf Johann Cord Rüter (1936) 'Benbow's Grand National Holiday' in *International Review of Social History* Volume 1, 1936, Leiden, p.217.

51. E.P. Thompson (1968) *The Making of the English Working Class,* Penguin, London, p.898.

52. See Paul Foot (2005), p.86.

53. E.P. Thompson (1968), p.898.

54. Quoted in E.P. Thompson (1968), p.892.

55. See John Saville (1994), p 73.

56. John Saville (1994), p.81.

57. Frederick Engels (1987) *The Condition of the Working Class in*

England, Penguin, London, p.243.

58. Thomas Babington Macaulay (1831) 'Speech on The Reform Bill of 1832', *Modern History Sourcebook*, Fordham University, available at https://sourcebooks.fordham.edu/mod/1832macaulay-reform.asp

59. Antonio Gramsci (1971) *Selections from the Prison Notebooks*, Quintin Hoare and Geoffrey Nowell Smith (eds) Lawrence and Wishart, London, p.80.

60. Walter Bagehot (1894) *The English Constitution,* Kegan Paul, Trench, Trubner and Co., London, p.xxiii. Bagehot quoted in Saville (1994), p.28.

61. Quoted in Trygve Tholfsen (1976) *Working Class Radicalism in Mid-Victorian England*, Croom Helm, London, p.210.

62. Quoted in Trygve Tholfsen (1976), p.204.

63. Quoted in Trygve Tholfsen (1976), p.214.

64. Robert Gray (1981) *The Aristocracy of Labour in Nineteenth Century Britain*, Macmillan, London, p.45.

65. Peter Clarke (1971) *Lancashire and the New Liberalism,* Cambridge University Press, Cambridge, p.321.

66. David Nicholls (1988), 'A Subordinate Bourgeoisie? The Question of Hegemony in Modern British Capitalist Society', in Colin Barker and David Nicholls (eds), *The Development of British Capitalist Society*, Northern Marxists Historians Group, Manchester, p.49.

67. See Paul Foot (2005), p.158.

68. L.T. Hobhouse, 'Liberalism' in Alan Bullock and Maurice Shock (eds) (1956) *The Liberal Tradition: From Fox to Keynes*, Clarendon, Oxford, p.214.

69. Laura Trevelyan (2012) A Very British Family: The Trevelyans and Their World, I.B. Tauris, London.

70. Tom Ling (1998) *The British State Since 1945: An Introduction,* Polity, Cambridge, p.21.

71. Figures from, Kingsley Bryce Smellie (1950) *A Hundred Years of British Government,* Duckworth, London, pp.162 and 328.

72. John Scott (1991) *Who Rules Britain?* Polity, Cambridge, p.128

73. John Scott (1991), p.135

74. Karl Marx (1864) 'Inaugural Address to the International Working Men's Association', in Karl Marx, *The First International and After*, David Fernbach (ed), Penguin, London, p.78.

75. Roy Church (1975) *The Great Victorian Boom 1850-1873*, Macmillan, London, p.72.

76. Robert Gray (1981) *The Aristocracy of Labour in Nineteenth Century Britain*, Macmillan, London, p.45.

77. Chris Bambery (1998) 'Myth and Reality in British Working Class Struggle', in John Rees (ed), *Essays on Historical Materialism*, Bookmarks, London, p.137.

78. Timothy Parsons (1999) *The British Imperial Century, 1815–1914: A World History Perspective*, Rowman & Littlefield, London, p.3

79. G.D.H. Cole, and Raymond Postgate (1961) *The Common People*, London, Methuen, London, p.404.

80. Tom Ling (1998) *The British State Since 1945: An Introduction*, Polity, Cambridge, p.19.

81. Leon Trotsky (2008) *History of the Russian Revolution*, Haymarket, Chicago, p.74.

82. For a very careful assessment of the impact of racist ideas in the age of empire see Satnam Virdee (2014) *Racism, Class and the Racialized Outsider*, Palgrave Macmillan, London, ch 3 and 4.

83. Perry Anderson (1964) 'Origins of the Current Crisis', *New Left Review* 1/23, Jan/ Feb 1964, p.36.

84. Chris Bambery (1998), p.138.

85. Satnam Virdee (2014), p.37.

86. Quoted in Paul Foot (2005), p.163/4.

87. Quoted in Paul Foot (2005), p.139/140.

88. Quoted in Paul Foot (2005), p.142.

89. Quotes in Paul Foot (2005), p.143.
90. Donna Torr (1957) *Tom Mann and His Times*, Lawrence and Wishart, London, p.279.
91. Frederick Engels (1889) Engels To Eduard Bernstein, *Marx Engels Correspondence*, Available at http://www.marxists.org/archive/marx/works/1889/letters/89_08_22.htm
92. A.L. Morton (1938) *A People's History of England*, Gollancz, London, p.437.
93. Quoted in Tony Cliff (1988) The Labour Party: A Marxist History, Bookmarks, London, p.25.
94. What Socialism is (1890) *Fabian tract* No 13, Fabians, London p.3. Available at https://digital.library.lse.ac.uk/objects/lse:lis607taw/read/single#page/2/mode/2up
95. Quoted in Ralph Miliband (2009) *Parliamentary Socialism: A Study in the Politics of Labour*, Merlin, Pontypool.
96. Eric Hobsbawm (1987), *Industry and Empire: 1875-1914*, Weidenfield and Nicholson, London, p.240.
97. Stuart Hall (1984) 'The Rise of the Representative/Interventionist State' in Gregor McLennan, David Held and Stuart Hall (eds) (1984) *State and Society in Contemporary Britain*, Polity Press, Cambridge, p.40.
98. Chanie Rosenberg (1987) *1919: Britain on the Brink of Revolution*, Bookmarks, London, p.30.
99. D.S. Morton (1919) *The 40 Hours Strike: An Historic Survey of the First General Strike in Scotland*, Clydebank Branch of SLP, Glasgow, p.6.
100. Chanie Rosenberg (1987), p.39.
101. Quoted in Donny Gluckstein (1985) *The Western Soviets: Workers' Councils Versus Parliament 1915-1920*, Bookmarks, London, p.85.
102. G.W. Reynolds and A. Judge (1968) *The Night the Police Went on Strike*, London p.4
103. Andrew Rothstein (1985) *The Soldiers' Strikes of 1919*, Journeyman, London, p.35.

104. Chanie Rosenberg (1987), p.14.

105. G.W. Reynolds and A. Judge (1968), p.68.

106. Chanie Rosenberg (1987), p.67

107. Quoted in Allen Hutt (1937) *The Post War History of the British Working Class*, Left Book Club, London, pp.18-19.

108. According to Winston Churchill the strike, 'was averted by the good sense of all concerned and notably by the assistance of rendered by many Honourable Gentlemen sitting on the benches directly opposite'. Quoted in Chanie Rosenberg (1987), p.67.

109. Allen Hutt (1937), p.21.

110. See Tony Cliff (1988), p.89.

111. G.D.H. Cole quoted in Ralph Miliband (2009), p.89.

112. Ralph Miliband (2009), p.110.

113. Ralph Miliband (2009), p.108.

114. For a full account of this episode, see W.P. and Z.K. Coates (1948) *A History of Anglo-Soviet Relations*, Lawrence and Wishart, London, ch 8.

115. W.H. Crook (1931) *The General Strike*, Oxford University Press, Oxford, p.419.

116. W.H. Crook (1931), p.415.

117. J.C.W. Reith (1949) *Into the Wind*, Hodder and Stoughton, London, p.108. As Reith records on pp 111-112 as a result of this partisan position, during the strike the BBC refused to let the Archbishop of Canterbury appeal for negotiations or Ramsay MacDonald make a broadcast.

118. Emile Burns (1926) *The General Strike, May, 1926: Trades Councils in Action*, Labour Research Department, London, p.111.

119. See Ralph Miliband (2009), p.141.

120. Quoted in Ralph Miliband (2009), p.143.

121. Stuart Hall (1984), p.44.

122. Quoted in Foot (2005), p.308.

123. Harold Laski (1943) *Reflections on the Revolution of Our*

Times, Viking, New York.

124. Quoted in Paul Addison (1975) *The Road to 1945,* Pimlico, London, pp.154-155.

125. Quoted in Paul Addison (1975), p.217.

126. W.K. Hancock, and M.M. Gowing (1949) *The British War Economy,* Her Majesty's Stationery Office, London, p.297.

127. Quoted in Henry Pelling (1985) *A Short History of the Labour Party,* Macmillan, London, p.96.

128. E.E. Barry (1965) *Nationalisation in British Politics,* Cape, London, p.68.

129. See John Campbell (1987) *Nye Bevan and the Mirage of British Socialism,* Norton, London, p.168.

130. See, for example, Sir Stafford Cripps' comments that 'until there are more workers on the managerial side of industry I think it would be almost impossible to have worker-controlled industry in Britain, even if it were on the whole desirable'. Quoted in Paul Foot (2005), p.324.

131. Paul Foot (2005), p.325.

132. Quoted in H. Mercer (1991), p.84.

133. Tom Ling (1998), p.28.

134. Tom Ling (1998), p.29.

135. Andrew Davies (1996) *To Build A New Jerusalem,* Abacus, London, pp 225-226.

136. Paul Foot quotes Harold Wilson saying, 'I was more than a little surprised, at the sudden hostility that blew up.' See Paul Foot (2005), p.337.

137. Quoted in Tony Cliff (1988), p.57.

138. Quoted in Tony Cliff p.243.

139. See Simon Hannah (2018), p.85, and Tony Cliff (1988), p.233.

140. Even in its first years, the Attlee government barely attempted to implement Keynesian policies, and 'quickly bowed to the pressures of economic orthodoxy in the difficult post-war conditions', Dominic Alexander (2018) *The Limits of Keynesianism,* Counterfire, London, p.56.

141. See Tony Cliff (1988), p.232.
142. Ralph Darlington and Dave Lyddon (2001) *Glorious Summer: Class Struggle in Britain 1972*. Bookmarks, London, p.209.
143. February 1974 Labour Party Manifesto, *Let us Work Together – Labour's Way out of the Crisis*. Available at http://www.labour-party.org.uk/manifestos/1974/feb/1974-feb-labour-manifesto.shtml
144. Paul Foot (2005), p.378.
145. Tony Benn (2005) *The Benn Diaries 1940-1990*, Random House, London, pp.302 and 287.
146. Tony Benn (2005), p.291.
147. Paul Foot (2005), p.380.
148. Tony Benn (2005), p.451.
149. Paul Foot (2005), p.381.
150. Chris Bambery (1986) *Ireland's Permanent Revolution*, Bookmarks, London, p.69.
151. Paul Hirst (1994) *Associative Democracy: New Forms of Economic and Social Governance*, Polity, Cambridge, p.86.
152. Tony Benn (2005), p.320.
153. Quoted in Paul Foot (2005), p.388.
154. Quoted in Cliff (1988), p.322.
155. Quoted in Cliff (1988), p.332.
156. See Ralph Darlington and Dave Lyddon (2001), p.226.
157. See Paul Foot (2005), p.396.
158. J. Hughes (1979) 'Public expenditure, the retreat from Keynes'. In Coates, K (ed) *What Went Wrong*, Spokesman, Nottingham, p.105.
159. Maurice Saatchi interviewed in *Thatcher: A Very British Revolution*, BBC, first shown
160. The Centre for Policy Studies, https://www.cps.org.uk/about/
161. Thatcher's motto, 'There is no alternative' seems to have first appeared in a Daily Telegraph article she wrote on 22 May 1980. Her 'You can't buck the market comment' comes from

a 1988 speech to parliament, see *Hansard*, 10 March 1988, https://api.parliament.uk/historic-hansard/commons/1988/mar/10/engagements#S6CV0129P0_19880310_HOC_156

162. See Andrew Jowett & Michael Hardie (2014) *Longer-term trends - Public Sector Finance*, Office of National Statistics, available at: https://webarchive.nationalarchives.gov.uk/20160105193307/http://www.ons.gov.uk/ons/rel/elmr/longer-term-trends/public-sector-fianaces/art-ltt-psf.html For more detail on the trends since the early nineties see *The Treasury Statistical Bulletin: Public Spending Statistics* April 2015, available at:
https://assets.publishing.service.gov.uk/government/uploads/system/uploads/attachment_data/file/424836/PSS_April_2015.pdf

163. Stephen Gill (2015) *Global Organic Crisis and Geopolitics*. Available at http://stephengill.com/news/2015/08/global-organic-crisis-and-geopolitics.html

164. Simon Clarke (1988) *Keynesianism, Monetarism and the Crisis of the State*, Edward Elgar, London, p.1 and p.329.

165. Quoted in William Mitchell and Thomas Fazi (2017) *Reclaiming the State: A Progressive Vision of Sovereignty for a Post-Neoliberal World*, Pluto, London, p.53.

166. Ipsos MORI, *Margaret Thatcher: Public Opinion Trends*, 8 April 2013, available at: https://ems.ipsos-mori.com/researchpublications/researcharchive/3158/Margaret-Thatcher-19252013.aspx

167. *Report of Nationalised Industries Policy Group (leaked Ridley report)*, Thatcher MSS, 2/6/1/37, available at: https://www.margaretthatcher.org/document/110795

168. Financial Times, 1 December 1983, quoted in Audrey Farrell (1992) *Crime Class and Corruption: The politics of the Police*, Bookmarks, London, p.92.

169. Seumas Milne, 'During the miners' strike, Thatcher's secret state was the real enemy within'. *The Guardian*, 3 October

2014.

170. Alan Travis, 'Thatcher had secret plan to use army at height of miners' strike', *The Guardian*, 13 January, 2003.

171. The argument went that workers had been bought off by improved lifestyles, share ownership and consumer choice, even though the number of people below the poverty line was going up throughout the period. For Stuart Hall, one of the most eloquent of the critics of Thatcherism, the new consumerism was in danger of burying class consciousness altogether:

'In a world saturated by money exchange, and everywhere mediated by money, the 'market' experience is *the* most immediate, daily and universal experience of the economic system for everyone...it should not surprise us if the mass of working people don't possess the concepts with which to cut into the process at another point, frame another set of questions, and bring to the surface or reveal what the overwhelming facticity of the market constantly renders invisible.'

Stuart Hall (1996) 'The Problem of Ideology, Marxism without Guarantees' in David Morley and Kuan-Hsing Chen (eds), *Stuart Hall: Critical Dialogues in Cultural Studies*, Routledge, London, p.38.

172. Neil Kinnock (1986) *Making Our Way*, Basil Blackwell, London, p.56.

173. Financial Times, 23 July, 1986. Quoted in Tony Cliff (1988), p.360.

174. Mike Wayne (2018) *England's Discontents: Political Cultures and National Identities*, Pluto, London, p.176.

175. Quoted by George Parker, 'Fiscal Focus', *Financial Times*, 7 December 2009.

176. Colin Leys (2014) 'The British Ruling Class', in *Socialist Register*, Volume 50, Merlin, London, p.111.

177. Costas Lapavitsas (2013) *Profiting Without Producing*, Verso,

London p.337 and ff.

178. See William Mitchell and Thomas Fazi (2018), p.139.

179. David Walker and John Tizard (2018) 'Out of Contract: Time to move on from the 'love in' with outsourcing and PFI', *London Smith Institute*, p.5.

180. David Walker and John Tizard (2018), p.5.

181. George Monbiot (2001) *The Captive State: The Corporate Takeover of Britain*, Macmillan, London.

182. David Beetham and Stuart Weir (1999) 'Auditing British Democracy', *Political Quarterly*, Blackwell, Oxford p.232.

183. Tom Ling (1998), p.132.

184. Trevor Smith (2003) 'Something Old, Something New, Something Borrowed, Something Blue: Themes of Tony Blair and his Government', *Parliamentary Affairs*, Volume 56, No. 4, p.588.

185. Colin Leys (2014), p.129.

186. Colin Leys (2014), p.129.

187. Colin Leys (2014), p.130.

188. Colin Leys (2014), p.129.

189. Martin Williams, 'FactCheck Q&A: How Posh is Parliament?' *Channel Four News*, 20 June 2017, available at https://www.channel4.com/news/factcheck/factcheck-qa-how-posh-is-parliament

190. Tom O'Grady (2018) 'Careerists versus Coal-Miners: Welfare Reforms and the Substantive Representation of Social Groups in the British Labour Party'. Unpublished Research, April 24, 2018, available at: http://discovery.ucl.ac.uk/10052651/1/careerists%20coal%20miners_final.pdf

191. Damian McBride (2013) *Power Trip: A Decade of Policy, Plots and Spin,* Biteback Publishing, London, p.414.

192. Herman E. Daly, 'The Perils of Free Trade', *Scientific American*, November 1993, Quoted in William Mitchell and Thomas Fazi (2017), p.121.

193. Stephen Gill (2000) 'Theoretical Foundations of a Neo-

Gramsican Analysis of European Integration' in H.J. Bieling
and J. Steinhilber (eds) *Dimensions of a Critical Theory of
European Integration*, FEG, Marburg, pp.15-33.

194. Quoted in William Mitchell and Thomas Fazi (2017), p.143.
195. Quoted in William Mitchell and Thomas Fazi (2017), p.145.
196. David Cameron, 'Speech to Lord Mayor's Banquet'
15 November 2010, available at: https://www.gov.uk/
government/speeches/speech-to-lord-mayors-banquet
197. Bill Lehane, 'U.K. Reportedly Seeks Military Bases in
Caribbean and Asia', *Bloomberg*, December 2018, available
at: 30 December 2018, 12:51 GMT https://www.bloomberg.
com/news/articles/2018-12-30/u-k-seeks-military-bases-in-
caribbean-and-asia-telegraph-says
198. Alannah Breeze, 'International perspective on UK foreign
direct investment (FDI):2014' *Office for National Statistics*,
30 August 2016, available at: https://www.ons.gov.uk/
economy/nationalaccounts/balanceofpayments/articles/
internationalperspectiveonukforeigndirectinvestmentfdi/2014
199. Jessica Elgot, 'UK 'living a lie' on defence capability, says
former army chief', *The Guardian*, 26 June 2018.

It is important to recognise here that in general it is foreign
policy that drives militarism and the large-scale investment
in the arms industry, not the other way around. This is
generally true of the arms race under capitalism and was
pointed out by the Russian Marxist economist Bukharin
in the run up to World War One: 'Capitalist society is
unthinkable without armaments, as it is unthinkable
without wars. And just as it is true that not low prices cause
competition but, on the contrary, competition causes low
prices, it is equally true that not the existence of arms is
the prime cause and the moving force in wars (although
wars are obviously impossible without arms) but, on
the contrary, the inevitableness of economic conflicts
conditions the existence of arms. This is why in our times,

when economic conflicts have reached an unusual degree of intensity, we are witnessing a mad orgy of armaments.' Nikolai Bukharin (1987) *Imperialism and the World Economy*, Merlin Press, London, p.127.

200. Peter Hennessy (2004) 'The Lightning Flash on the Road to Baghdad: Issues of Evidence', in W.G. Runciman (ed), *Lifting the Lid on the Workings of Power*, Published for The British Academy by Oxford University Press, Oxford, p.70.

201. In Tom Mills book 'The BBC: Myth of a Public Service', Frank Gardner, the BBC's security correspondent is quoted admitting to close contact with MI5 and MI6. He admits too to applying for a job with MI6 and he appears to have acted as a go between for MI6 at the BBC following the death of David Kelly. Tom Mills (2016) *The BBC: Myth of a Public Service*, e-Book version, Verso, London, Loc 1023 of 5150.

202. Paul Carter, 'Could an Army coup remove Jeremy Corbyn – just as it almost toppled Harold Wilson?' *Daily Telegraph*, 9 May 2018.

203. Damien Gayle, 'Cambridge among partners shortlisted for £70m MoD funding, documents show.' *The Guardian*, 13 March 2019.

204. Damien Gayle, '£2m for Scottish firm to counter Russian propaganda did not go towards its social media, says Alan Duncan', *The Guardian*, 13 December 2018.

205. Spencer Ackerman and James Ball, 'Optic Nerve: millions of Yahoo webcam images intercepted by GCHQ', *The Guardian*, 28 February 2014.

206 'Public order and safety spending', *Institute for Fiscal Studies*, 29 September 2015, available at: https://www.ifs.org.uk/tools_and_resources/fiscal_facts/public_spending_survey/public_order_and_safety

207. Liz Fekete (2013) 'Total Policing: Reflections from the Frontline', *Race and Class*, Vol 54(3), p.72.

208. McCulloch J. and Pickering S. (2009) 'Pre-Crime and counter

terrorism: Imagining future crime in the "war on terror"', *British Journal of Criminology*, Vol 49 no 5. Quoted in Liz Fekete (2013), p.72.

209. Justin Schlosberg (2016) *Should he stay or should he go? Television and Online News Coverage of the Labour Party in Crisis*, Media Reform Society, p.4, available at: http://www.mediareform.org.uk/wp-content/uploads/2016/07/Corbynresearch.pdf

210. Jack Peat, 'Lawyer speaks out over BBC bias against Corbyn as evidence of "coded negative imagery" emerges', *The London Economic*, 12 December, 2018, available at: https://www.thelondoneconomic.com/news/lawyer-speaks-out-over-bbc-bias-against-corbyn-as-evidence-of-coded-negative-imagery-emerges/12/12/

211. Pierre Dardot and Christian Laval (2017) *The New Way of the World: On Neoliberal Society*, Verso, London, Loc 252.

212. Pierre Dardot and Christian Laval (2017) Loc 281.

213. Pierre Dardot and Christian Laval (2017) Loc 316.

214. Merryn Somerset Webb, 'A post-crisis cure that has stored up economic pain', *Financial Times,* 15/16 September 2018.

215. Istvan Meszaros (2010), p.135.

216. Susan Strange, *The Retreat of the State*, Cambridge University Press, Cambridge, p.45.

217. Paul Mason (2015) *PostCapitalism: A Guide to Our Future*, Allen Lane, London, p.8.

218. Paul Mason, 'After the storm: what should Corbynism 2.0 look like?', *New Statesman*, 17 August 2018, available at: https://www.newstatesman.com/politics/uk/2018/08/after-storm-what-should-corbynism-20-look

219. William Mitchell and Thomas Fazi (2017) ch. 10.

220. Leo Panitch and Sam Gindin, as above p.17.

221. Leo Panitch and Sam Gindin, as above p.19.

222. The importance of Poulantzas (amongst others) as an influence on this strand of left thinking is spelt out clearly

in Ed Rooksby (2018) "'Structural Reform' and the Problem of Socialist Strategy Today", *Critique*, Vol. 46, No. 1, pp.27-48. This is also one of the clearest and most thoughtful discussions of the 'in and against' strategy.

223. Nicos Poulantzas (2000) *State, Power, Socialism*, Verso, London, p.119.

224. Nicos Poulantzas (2000), p.256.

225. Istvan Meszaros (2010) *Historical Actuality of the Socialist Offensive: Alternative to Parliamentarism*, Bookmarks, London, p.104.

226. Quoted in Geoffrey Foote (1997) *The Labour Party's Political Thought: A History*, Macmillan, London, p.147.

227. Antonio Gramsci (1971) pp.60/61.

228. See Donny Gluckstein (1985) *The Western Soviets: Workers Councils Versus Parliament*, Bookmarks, London, p.120 and ff and p.162 and ff, Jeffrey Webber (2014) *The Last Day of Oppression, and the First Day of the Same: The Politics and Economics of the New Latin American Left*, Pluto, London, p.44, and Colin Barker (ed) (1987) *Revolutionary Rehearsals*, Bookmarks, London, Chapters 2 and 3.

229. Donny Gluckstein (1985), p.194.

230. Jacques Danos and Marcel Gibelin (1986) *June '36: Class Struggle and the Popular Front in France*, Bookmarks, London, p.145.

231. 'Labour could renationalise railways in five years – McDonnell', *BBC Website*, 22 September 2018.

232. Karl Marx (1975) 'On the Jewish Question', in *Marx: Early Writings*, Pelican, London, p.220.

CULTURE, SOCIETY & POLITICS

The modern world is at an impasse. Disasters scroll across our smartphone screens and we're invited to like, follow or upvote, but critical thinking is harder and harder to find. Rather than connecting us in common struggle and debate, the internet has sped up and deepened a long-standing process of alienation and atomization. Zer0 Books wants to work against this trend.
With critical theory as our jumping off point, we aim to publish books that make our readers uncomfortable. We want to move beyond received opinions.
Zer0 Books is on the left and wants to reinvent the left. We are sick of the injustice, the suffering, and the stupidity that defines both our political and cultural world, and we aim to find a new foundation for a new struggle.

If this book has helped you to clarify an idea, solve a problem or extend your knowledge, you may want to check out our online content as well. Look for Zer0 Books: Advancing Conversations in the iTunes directory and for our Zer0 Books YouTube channel.

Popular videos include:

Žižek and the Double Blackmain

The Intellectual Dark Web is a Bad Sign

Can there be an Anti-SJW Left?

Answering Jordan Peterson on Marxism

Follow us on Facebook
at https://www.facebook.com/ZeroBooks and Twitter at https://twitter.com/Zer0Books

Bestsellers from Zer0 Books include:

Give Them An Argument
Logic for the Left
Ben Burgis
Many serious leftists have learned to distrust talk of logic. This is
a serious mistake.
Paperback: 978-1-78904-210-8 ebook: 978-1-78904-211-5

Poor but Sexy
Culture Clashes in Europe East and West
Agata Pyzik
How the East stayed East and the West stayed West.
Paperback: 978-1-78099-394-2 ebook: 978-1-78099-395-9

An Anthropology of Nothing in Particular
Martin Demant Frederiksen
A journey into the social lives of meaninglessness.
Paperback: 978-1-78535-699-5 ebook: 978-1-78535-700-8

In the Dust of This Planet
Horror of Philosophy vol. 1
Eugene Thacker
In the first of a series of three books on the Horror of Philosophy,
In the Dust of This Planet offers the genre of horror as a way of
thinking about the unthinkable.
Paperback: 978-1-84694-676-9 ebook: 978-1-78099-010-1

The End of Oulipo?
An Attempt to Exhaust a Movement
Lauren Elkin, Veronica Esposito
Paperback: 978-1-78099-655-4 ebook: 978-1-78099-656-1

Capitalist Realism
Is There no Alternative?
Mark Fisher
An analysis of the ways in which capitalism has presented itself
as the only realistic political-economic system.
Paperback: 978-1-84694-317-1 ebook: 978-1-78099-734-6

Rebel Rebel
Chris O'Leary
David Bowie: every single song. Everything you want to know,
everything you didn't know.
Paperback: 978-1-78099-244-0 ebook: 978-1-78099-713-1

Kill All Normies
Angela Nagle
Online culture wars from 4chan and Tumblr to Trump.
Paperback: 978-1- 78535-543-1 ebook: 978-1-78535-544-8

Cartographies of the Absolute
Alberto Toscano, Jeff Kinkle
An aesthetics of the economy for the twenty-first century.
Paperback: 978-1-78099-275-4 ebook: 978-1-78279-973-3

Malign Velocities
Accelerationism and Capitalism
Benjamin Noys
Long listed for the Bread and Roses Prize 2015, *Malign Velocities*
argues against the need for speed, tracking acceleration
as the symptom of the ongoing crises of capitalism.
Paperback: 978-1-78279-300-7 ebook: 978-1-78279-299-4

Meat Market
Female Flesh under Capitalism
Laurie Penny
A feminist dissection of women's bodies as the fleshy fulcrum of
capitalist cannibalism, whereby women are both consumers and
consumed.
Paperback: 978-1-84694-521-2 ebook: 978-1-84694-782-7

Babbling Corpse
Vaporwave and the Commodification of Ghosts
Grafton Tanner
Paperback: 978-1-78279-759-3 ebook: 978-1-78279-760-9

New Work New Culture
Work we want and a culture that strengthens us
Frithjoff Bergmann
A serious alternative for mankind and the planet.
Paperback: 978-1-78904-064-7 ebook: 978-1-78904-065-4

Romeo and Juliet in Palestine
Teaching Under Occupation
Tom Sperlinger
Life in the West Bank, the nature of pedagogy and the role of a
university under occupation.
Paperback: 978-1-78279-637-4 ebook: 978-1-78279-636-7

Ghosts of My Life
Writings on Depression, Hauntology and Lost Futures
Mark Fisher
Paperback: 978-1-78099-226-6 ebook: 978-1-78279-624-4

Sweetening the Pill
or How We Got Hooked on Hormonal Birth Control
Holly Grigg-Spall
Has contraception liberated or oppressed women?
Sweetening the Pill breaks the silence on the dark side of hormonal
contraception.
Paperback: 978-1-78099-607-3 ebook: 978-1-78099-608-0

Why Are We The Good Guys?
Reclaiming your Mind from the Delusions of Propaganda
David Cromwell
A provocative challenge to the standard ideology that Western
power is a benevolent force in the world.
Paperback: 978-1-78099-365-2 ebook: 978-1-78099-366-9

The Writing on the Wall
On the Decomposition of Capitalism and its Critics
Anselm Jappe, Alastair Hemmens
A new approach to the meaning of social emancipation.
Paperback: 978-1-78535-581-3 ebook: 978-1-78535-582-0

Enjoying It
Candy Crush and Capitalism
Alfie Bown
A study of enjoyment and of the enjoyment of studying. Bown
asks what enjoyment says about us and what we say about
enjoyment, and why.
Paperback: 978-1-78535-155-6 ebook: 978-1-78535-156-3

Color, Facture, Art and Design
Iona Singh
This materialist definition of fine-art develops guidelines for
architecture, design, cultural-studies and ultimately social
change.
Paperback: 978-1-78099-629-5 ebook: 978-1-78099-630-1

Neglected or Misunderstood
The Radical Feminism of Shulamith Firestone
Victoria Margree
An interrogation of issues surrounding gender, biology,
sexuality, work and technology, and the ways in which our
imaginations continue to be in thrall to ideologies of maternity
and the nuclear family.
Paperback: 978-1-78535-539-4 ebook: 978-1-78535-540-0

How to Dismantle the NHS in 10 Easy Steps (Second Edition)
Youssef El-Gingihy
The story of how your NHS was sold off and why you will have
to buy private health insurance soon. A new expanded second
edition with chapters on junior doctors' strikes and government
blueprints for US-style healthcare.
Paperback: 978-1-78904-178-1 ebook: 978-1-78904-179-8

Digesting Recipes
The Art of Culinary Notation
Susannah Worth
A recipe is an instruction, the imperative tone of the expert, but
this constraint can offer its own kind of potential. A recipe need
not be a domestic trap but might instead offer escape – something
to fantasise about or aspire to.
Paperback: 978-1-78279-860-6 ebook: 978-1-78279-859-0

Most titles are published in paperback and as an ebook.
Paperbacks are available in traditional bookshops. Both print and
ebook formats are available online.
Follow us on Facebook
at https://www.facebook.com/ZeroBooks
and Twitter at https://twitter.com/Zer0Books